1 2 3 4 5 6 7 8 9 0

Kī Hō'alu

Learn to Play Hawaiian Slack Key Guitar

by
Keola Beamer
and
Mark Nelson

Online Audio

www.melbay.com/96695BCDEB

Audio Contents

I0809694

Cover Credit: (Beamer Model) Grimes Guitar Co., Kula, Hawaii.

Visit us on the Web at http://www.melbay.com — E-mail us at email @ melbay.com

Aloha

For many years *Kī Hō'alu* has been passed down from father to son in a way that is typical for Island folks. When the house is quiet and the day's work is done, the father takes his old guitar out of its battered case. Moving to the back porch, he finds a favorite chair, stretches out his tired legs, and cradles the instrument gently in his arms. The young boy's face lights up in wonder as a sweet sounding melody fills the warm evening.

It is difficult to explain, but I believe this to be the defining moment of our music. This silk in the air. It is what we Hawaiians call *nahenahe*. Soft, soothing, satisfying music. The kind of music that swells up in your heart like a big blue wave. The kind of music that whispers in your soul. The kind of music that accepts your cares and troubles and dims them down, like the fading light on the old man's porch.

This is how I learned to play the Hawaiian Slack Key Guitar. I was sitting with my grandfather on a tiny little island in the middle of the Pacific and I began to hear that beautiful whispering.

I first met Mark Nelson when I invited him to my *la hanau* (birthday) in 1996. We sat together on the front porch of a beach house on the Kona coast of the Big Island of *Hawai'i*. Mark was then known to me as a successful author of musical instruction books, but I really didn't know much about his playing or his feel for the music. I just knew that he wrote good books. Mark took out a sweet looking *koa* guitar and started to play. A solo instrumental performance gives no place to hide. One can give interviews to famous guitar magazines and write books until the cows come home, but sitting here playing *kī hō'alu* for Keola Beamer and his family on the remarkable island of their ancestors, well...

My wife and I looked at each other. My mother put down her *lei* needle. My brother Kaliko, who was weaving a coconut hat, had grown a big smile on his face. We didn't have to say it, but we all thought it on that bright afternoon.

Nahenahe...

So Mark and I became good friends and decided to write this book. We wanted to write a method book that would give you the tools to find the music in your own heart. To create the music with your own hands. To give *you* a chance to make the music that whispers.

Come and sit on the porch.

Keola Beamer

Kona, Hawaii 1997

Foreword

Hawaiian Slack Key Guitar (***Kī Hō'alu***) is one of the world's great acoustic guitar traditions. This tradition includes virtuoso guitar pieces, but the majority of songs played slack key are classic Hawaiian melodies either played as instrumentals or as accompaniment to vocals with instrumental breaks between the verses. Slack key does not mean a type of guitar—rather, it is any guitar played slack key style.

This beautiful tradition began back around 1832, about 60 years before the steel guitar came along. At first the slack key guitar was used almost exclusively to accompany the voice. A wide variety of tunings in several different keys were created to back up the singers effectively. Hawaiians retuned the guitar from the standard Spanish tuning (E-A-D-G-B-E, from lowest to highest pitched string), resulting in sweet sounding tunings with "slacked" strings.

The many ingenious tunings the Hawaiians invented fall into five basic categories: **Major** (a tuning that is a major chord or contains a major chord); ***Wahine*** (a tuning that contains a major 7th note); ***Mauna Loa*** (a tuning where the two highest strings are tuned a fifth apart); ***Ni'ihau/Old Mauna Loa*** (a tuning where the second and sixth notes of the scale lie on two successive strings with the sixth note of the scale on the lower-pitched string); and Miscellaneous (many other combinations that don't fit readily into one of these groupings). The first three categories; **Major, *Wahine***, and ***Mauna Loa***, are the ones most often used and are represented in this great book. There are also six families of keys for these tunings: G, C, D, F, B♭, and A. All of these keys, except the key of A, are represented in this book.

The most influential slack key guitarist in history was the late Philip "Gabby" Pahinui (1921-1980), who is often referred to as the father of the modern slack key era because he made the first ever slack key recordings in 1946. He expanded the boundaries of slack key guitar, creating a fully evolved solo guitar style capable of interpreting a whole variety of Hawaiian traditional songs, popular standards, and original pieces. As stated earlier, in the beginning the slack key guitar was mainly used to accompany the vocals; but since Gabby's first recordings, some of which were instrumental, it has blossomed into a full-blown instrumental tradition which continues to expand now in the 1990's.

The slack key tradition is one of the roots of mainland American Country music, since the pedal steel guitar came from the lap steel, which came from the acoustic steel, which came from the slack key guitar. The slack key guitar and the classic Hawaiian music tradition can have the emotional depth of the blues, but has more emphasis on melody.

Keola Beamer and Mark Nelson have put together this wonderful instruction book. Based on arrangements by Keola and Mark, it is another great means for preserving this most beautiful tradition. Keola Beamer put out the first ever instruction book on slack key in 1973, recently he released an instructional video on Homespun. He has been performing, teaching, and recording since the early 70's, and is one of the greatest and most influential slack key guitarists in history. Mark Nelson has been involved in recording and teaching in various traditions, including old time Appalachian music, Irish music, and Hawaiian slack key for many years. It is great that they and Mel Bay Publications have worked together in putting out this beautiful instruction manual.

Aloha,
George "Keoki" Winston

Table Of Contents

Mahalo

I'd like to acknowledge the *mana'o* of Nona Beamer (my Mom) and Randy Fong, of the Performing Arts Center of the Kamehameha Schools. I am also grateful for the patience of my beautiful wife, Moanalani, a hula dancer who thinks it's pretty cool to hang with the band. *Mahalo* to Ozzie Kotani for his insight and companionship, also to my friend George Winston of Dancing Cat Records, for his love and support of my work. I appreciate my brother Kaliko Beamer-Trapp, who despite his busy schedule is always there for me to proofread manuscripts and translate.

Hawaiians like to grind (eat), and the *'ono kaukau* my student Nobu Yoshida makes for me when I am working in Lahaina is eminently grindable. *Mahalo* Nobu for your melodious guitar playing and for never asking me to wash the pots in the lunch wagon in the summertime, when it's really hot.

I especially appreciate the spirit of aloha and respect for our culture and traditions that Mark Nelson has brought to this project. We have spent many hours together with our pencils and tablature, trying to notate the stuff, to pass it on to future generations. It takes a bit of courage to help hold open the door of our world. *Mahalo* Mark and Annie for seeing this through.

Keola Beamer

Thank You

Writing a book requires support and help from far more people than those whose names appear on the cover. Raymond Kāne helped start me on my way to slack key, beginning with his long-distance call to a complete stranger in Oregon: *"Aloha from Hawai'i!"* His music and generosity have long been an inspiration. Bruddah Matt Manewa and Leabert Lindsey, of Kailua, Kona, Hawai'i made me feel right at home on my first trip to that beautiful island. We played and sang everything from slack key to cowboy music to doo wop. Ate good, too! Thanks as well to Kaliko for insight into the Hawaiian language, and to Nona Beamer, the soul of graciousness and hospitality. And *mahalo* to Larry Francis for his insight into the *English* language—a good proofreader is hard to find.

I would like to offer particular thanks to my collaborator, Keola Beamer, and his lovely wife Moana, whose love and friendship is an unexpectedly pleasant bonus. And to Annie, who thinks it's just fine that I sit around on the porch and play my guitar.

Mark Nelson

Introduction

Kī Hō'alu, or Hawaiian Slack Key Guitar, is both a way to play the guitar and a body of songs and unique tunings developed in the Hawaiian Islands over the past one hundred and fifty years. For many years, it remained mostly a rural, family-centered art. By the midpoint of the twentieth century, slack key was in danger of dying out, another old time tradition falling to the conformity of the modern world. Then came a series of ground-breaking recordings by the great Gabby Pahinui. His influence cannot be overstated; a number of contemporary master musicians like Raymond Kāne, Leonard Kwan and Sonny Chillingworth credit his recording of the song ***Hi'ilawe*** with their decision to keep playing!

Until just a few years ago, you had to go to Hawai'i to hear slack key. And even then you had to be very lucky; because the hotels and restaurants wouldn't feature it, the radio didn't play it, and recordings were few and far between. Slack key was country music, played around kerosene lanterns on the porch after the work was done. No one really took it seriously; and because of that, it was in serious danger of disappearing.

In 1973, a young Hawaiian musician named Keola Beamer published the *First Method for Hawaiian Slack Key Guitar*. Rarely was a book so aptly titled: Keola was literally the very first to pass on the tunings and stylings to the general public. The situation since then has changed considerably: in the Islands, on the Mainland, and indeed, around the world, *kī hō'alu* is entering a new golden age.

About This Book

No single book can ever substitute for the real experience of living in a musical tradition. But we feel that you will go a long way toward finding your own style of slack key guitar by following us through these pages. In many ways, Keola and Mark may be the ideal tutors—one was born of a centuries-old family of Hawaiian singers, dancers and chanters, the other simply followed his love of the music to the Islands. Both share the conviction that slack key is simply the *right* way to play the guitar.

The book is organized in four main sections. In the first, we introduce the most common tuning, and present a number of fairly easy songs. Next, we discuss how you might go about building your own arrangement and illustrate the process with a pair of more complex transcriptions. Section three is devoted to presenting some of the variety of slack key tunings and stylings. And finally, we present a selection of duets. Although the material is somewhat graded in nature, feel free to skip around.

What you need to play slack key

Slack key guitar can be played on any style of guitar—there are proponents of both steel string and nylon string acoustics, and even some electric players! Although our book is intended for the intermediate finger-style guitarist, beginners are encouraged to jump in and get their feet wet.

Flatpickers with little or no fingerpicking experience should take the time to master ***Bruddah John***; a simple ditty that develops independence of your thumb and fingers.

Don't be shy, there is plenty here for both newcomers and old hands. And you don't have to send us any fish!

About the Arrangements

Just to set the record straight: this is not just a book of transcriptions from Keola Beamer's albums. We have included a generous handful of interesting arrangements of songs intimately associated with Keola. Some have been previously recorded, some are brand new. And we have included songs arranged to reflect the styles of some of the masters of the slack key guitar. There are even original pieces by Keola and Mark written expressly for this book. Whatever the source, the songs were selected to give you a taste of some of the vitality of slack key.

In Hawaiian music, the individual contribution of the artist is revered. This is easily seen in slack key; no two players will play the same song exactly alike. In fact, a guitarist may completely change an arrangement to reflect the mood of the moment! So how to write a slack key method? How do you teach a style that is so dependent on personality and not inscribe a set of arrangements that become set in stone?

After much thought, we decided that each arrangement would serve a variety of functions. First, of course, we wanted to present songs that are fun to play and that will open the door into the style. Second, we wanted to offer a good solid repertoire for the guitarist new to the genre. And lastly, we wanted to encourage you to experiment.

You'll notice that most of the music consists of a simple introduction, the body of the tune, and a coda. Rather than write out an extended piece with a long introduction, verses, variations, a bridge and a coda, we give you the tools to create your own arrangement. When you become more and more familiar with the material you will see how you can adapt licks from one song into another, or even move songs around into different tunings.

We've carried the same idea over to the CD, as well. In a few cases, the recording features an introduction, bridge, or solo section that is not notated. We wanted you to hear examples of how you could take the basic arrangement and make it your own. By applying the tools you have learned in this book, you will be able to easily come up with unique interpretations to express your feelings.

As you progress through to the more difficult tunes, don't forget to go back and apply your new skills to the arrangements you first mastered. This constant re-examination is critical to mastering a new skill. Even ***Bruddah John*** can swing if you know how!

Slack key is a personal method of playing the guitar. It's part of the Hawaiian spirit of aloha. Play from your heart, and your fingers will follow.

The History of Hawaiian Slack Key Guitar

Early Hawaiian culture was based on oral tradition. Important historical information such as genealogies, land divisions, and navigational information was preserved in the memories of living human beings and passed down from generation to generation in the form of detailed and complex chants. Some ancient Hawaiian creation chants are over two thousand lines long. The oral tradition is inherent in the structure of our culture, so for most of Hawai'i's true past there is little or no written documentation.

Although slack key, or *Kī Hō'alu* is a relatively new development in the music of Hawai'i, there is still very little historic information available concerning it. An outline of its history is largely an intelligent interpolation among a few known facts.

The first experiments with Hawaiian Slack Key guitar playing began in about 1832, after the first guitars were introduced to Hawai'i. The series of events leading up to its introduction reaches back to 1793. Midshipman George Vancouver had been in Hawai'i with Captain Cook in 1778 and 1779. He returned in 1793 as Captain George Vancouver in command of H.M.S. Discovery. Among other gifts for King Kamehameha the Great, Vancouver brought six Texas longhorn cows, a bull, four ewes and two rams. Kamehameha protected the animals by placing a *kapu*, or restriction, on them. The *kapu* remained in effect for years and the animals roamed freely in what is now the district of South Kohala on the Big Island of Hawai'i. As their numbers increased, these herds of wild cattle became an annoying problem. By 1813, they had multiplied into the thousands, trampling taro patches, destroying crops and on occasion attacking people. In 1832, Liholiho (King Kamehameha II) sent a high chief as an emissary to California and arranged to have some Spanish, Mexican, and Indian men dispatched to the Islands who could teach the Hawaiians how to manage the cattle population.

These cowboys arrived on the Big Island and began to instruct the Hawaiians in riding and roping. As my mentor, Auntie Alice Nāmakelua, mentioned "Along with their saddles, lariats, and horses, the *vaqueros* brought their guitars."

After long days of riding and roping on the slopes of *Mauna Kea*, the *vaqueros* would relax in the evening, strumming their guitars and singing the songs of their homeland. To the Hawaiians the guitar must have seemed a fascinating musical instrument, for most of the pre-western Hawaiian instruments were entirely percussive. (The exceptions were the *pū*, the conch shell, the *'ūkēkē*, which used the fiber of the *olanā* plant to produce a plucked sound and the *'ohe hano ihu*, the Hawaiian nose flute. Both the *'ūkēkē*, and the *'ohe hano ihu* were played for evening courtship serenades and thus promptly banned by the missionaries.)

Island cowboys, or *paniolo* (from the Spanish—*español*) watched and listened to the Spaniards intently enough to comprehend the basic mechanics of producing sound on the guitar. It is doubtful that they learned much about the structure of the music or the theory involved. Their days were occupied with the more practical tasks of learning to work the range. It is also generally accepted that their Spanish tutors stayed only a few months in Hawai'i.

A few guitars were left behind, sold or traded to Hawaiians, and shortly afterwards *paniolo* of the district were playing the guitar in a unique and wonderful way.

For most people it is difficult to learn to play an instrument merely by watching it being played. Since the *paniolo* had only a brief exposure to the Spanish guitar, the Hawaiians were in a position of having to invent a way of playing it almost on their own. The first problem that surfaced was how to tune the instrument.

A logical first step would be to tune the six strings in relation to each other so that they made a pleasant sound when struck together. As it turns out, this can be achieved by loosening or slacking some of the strings. One simple example would be to tune down from the standard EADGBE tuning to achieve a DADF♯AD or a D major chord. Hence the phrase "Slack Key" and the Hawaiian language equivalent, *Kī* (key) *Hō'alu* (to slacken, slack).

Once this was accomplished, the next step would be to locate the necessary chords to accompany a song. Since the post-missionary Hawaiian music of the 1830's rarely utilized minor chords, this step was easily accomplished with the technique of barreing, known to all styles of guitar playing. If the guitar is tuned to produce a major chord on the open strings, by holding down all the strings with one finger placed at the first fret, the player could produce the same major chord one half step higher. In this manner all the major chords could be found, with no real knowledge of music theory. Perhaps they simply played by ear, barreing the appropriate fret at the chord changes in the songs.

Another important consideration in the invention of the Hawaiian Slack Key Guitar was string tension. This idea, in my opinion, has never been addressed adequately. The *paniolo* clearly understood the fallibility of ropes under high tension. Given the rather serious lack of guitar strings in Hawai'i, if the strings were broken by attempting to tune too high—how could those strings be replaced? Instead of a wonderful guitar, the *paniolo* instead would have a really nice piece of firewood.

The early players might have selected a major tuning that matched the range of their voices. Then they found the major chords and accompanied themselves singing their favorite songs. As you can probably guess, it is not just strumming and barreing that produce the beautiful and evocative sounds of the *kī hō'alu*. Far from it. Plucking different strings with different fingers of the right hand and using the left hand to create detailed harmonies began a tremendous expansion of slack key technique. The resonant and characteristic alternating bass appeared. How each player used these different right- and left-hand possibilities determined his or her own unique style.

Kī hō'alu gradually spread from the Big Island of Hawai'i to the other islands in the Hawaiian chain, players adding to and developing in a unique way what had been learned from their father or mother, uncles or aunties, grandfather or grandmother.

It is likely that for a long time *kī hō'alu* was used primarily as an accompaniment to songs, for in the old days the words of popular songs were more important than the music. According to Alice Nāmakelua, the style of playing in the early 1900's was to select perhaps two chords and a right hand plucking pattern which could be used for several different pieces. Since then the slack key guitar has become much more of a solo instrument, and the technique has developed in richness and complexity while retaining its unique Hawaiian spirit.

Keola Beamer

This petroglyph of a *paniolo* roping a calf was incised on a boulder sometime after 1830. Other rock carvings, both ancient and modern, appear in various places throughout the book.

How to Read Tablature

All of the music is written in standard notation and Tablature for guitar. Tunings are given twice, once as the common name for the tuning, for example ***Taro Patch***, and again as pitches immediately to the left of the first line.

Tablature, or TAB, is an ancient system of musical notation in which lines represent the instrument's strings, starting with the highest string on top. Fingering positions are indicated by numbers. TAB doesn't give any indication of how long to hold each note; for that refer to the staff above the TAB. (If you are unfamiliar with standard musical notation, see page 14.) For example:

In this example you would play the open fifth string with your thumb at the same time as plucking the third string at the fourth fret. Then you'd play a double stop with the open fourth string and the first string at the fifth fret. Pay attention to the direction of the note stems. Downward pointing stems are played with your thumb, upward pointing stems are sounded with your fingers.

Fingerings have not been indicated to allow each player to develop a personal style: experiment with different fingerings to see what works best for you. Although some old-time slack key players use only one or two fingers to sound the strings, Keola suggests learning to play with your index, middle and ring fingers for better tone and flexibility.

Here are some additional symbols you will encounter:

Slide: Play the first note, and slide up or down to the next. Try to sound each note clearly.

Hammer-on: Play the first note, then rapidly press your finger down to the fretboard to sound the second note.

Pull-off: Play the first note, then quickly pull off your finger to sound the lower note.

Hammer/pull combination: A common feature of slack key, this is a rapid combination of a hammer-on and pull-off executed as a quick flick of the finger. Slack key artists may combine hammers, pulls and slides (all technically called **slurs** in the music world) in bewildering variety. Mastery of these techniques is something so personal that an individual player can often be identified just from listening to the slurs.

Harmonic: Also called *chimes* in Hawaiian music. Lightly touch the string directly over the fret to produce a ringing tone. Keola recommends moving your plucking hand back towards the bridge slightly to better define the harmonic.

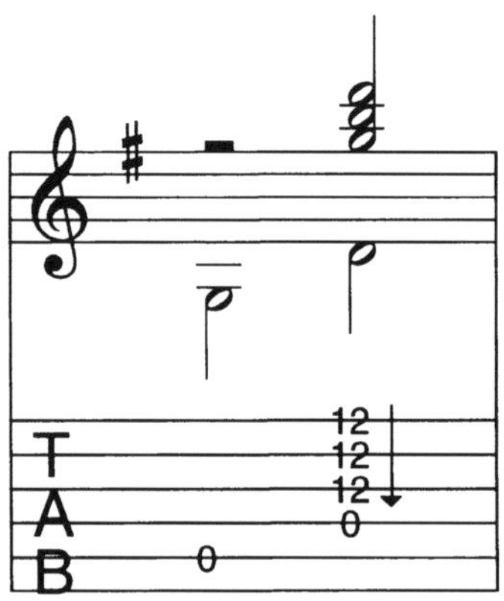

Brush: Brush upwards across the strings indicated with your index finger. An upward pointing arrow indicates a downward strum with your thumb.

Reading Musical Notation

Although it is not necessary to know how to read musical notation to play the songs in this book, knowledge of a few musical symbols will greatly enhance your enjoyment.

Since the TAB will give you the correct pitches on a properly tuned guitar, you really only have to worry about the rhythm of a particular piece.

Music is divided into **measures**, each of which contains the number of beats delineated by the **time signature:**

4/4 means four beats per measure, each quarter note counts as one beat.

3/4 is three beats per measure, each quarter note counts as one beat.

Occasionally alternate symbols are used for the time signature. **Cut Time** (¢) is another way of writing 2/2; and **Common Time** (C) is the same as 4/4.

Each beat can be further divided into smaller and smaller units:

The longest note is the whole note; it is the equivalent of four quarter notes, or four counts.

The half note is equal to two quarter notes.

The quarter note gets one count.

Two eighth notes equals a quarter note.

The sixteenth note is half as long as the eighth note; so two sixteenths equal one eighth, four sixteenths equal a quarter, and sixteen equal a whole note.

Rests correspond to each of the different note values.

A dot placed next to a note (or rest) lengthens it by one half of its value. For example:

Ties are used for notes that are held for their combined values:

This figure would be held as long as three eighth notes.

Triplets are groups of three notes that are played in the space of two.

For example, three eighth note triplets 

would be played in the same amount of time as two eighth notes: 

A few more signs to help you find your way:

Repeat signs: repeat the enclosed phrase one time before going on to the next one. (Note that often the first section of a tune only has the sign at the end of the phrase; treat it just as if the first sign were there.)

1 — This sign means play the measures under the sign on the first time through and then go back to the beginning of the section. On the repeat you skip over the first ending and play the second ending.

BV— — — A barre symbol means to cover all of the strings with your index finger at the fret indicated by the Roman numeral, and hold the barre as long as indicated by the dotted line. A partial barre is indicated by the sign **1/2B.**

𝄐 — A **fermata** is the symbol to hold a note just a little longer than its value. It is used to add expression to your playing.

D.C. — From the Italian, **Da Capo**, meaning “Head.” This sign directs you to go back to the beginning of the music. **D.C. al Fine** directs you to play from the beginning to the designated end of the song. We use the Hawaiian word ***pau*** in place of the Italian ***fine***.

D.S. — **Dal Segno**, or “to the sign,” tells you to look for the symbol (𝄋) and play that section next rather than returning to the beginning. **D.S. al𝄌** means play from the sign to the coda sign, then jump to the coda.

𝄌 — A **Coda** sign is often used to mark the ending of the piece. When you see this sign, skip down to the section marked 𝄌 **Coda** to finish the song. Coda is Italian for "Tail," by the way.

Rit. — Also **Ritard.** Gradually slow the pace to bring the music to a graceful conclusion.

Pau — Hawaiian for "done." When you see the word ***pau***, you've finished.

A Lesson With Keola Beamer

In February of 1998, Mark and Keola sat down in Keola's studio in Lahaina, Maui, to discuss some of the finer aspects of guitar playing, developing a personal style, Hawaiian music and culture, and lunch. Excerpts from that conversation appear throughout this book. Keola's quotes are in italics, Mark's in plain type.

Does slack key require any specialized technique? Is there any particular way to hold the guitar?

I recommend that my students hold the guitar in the classical style. If you tilt the guitar out just a little bit it's a much more visual presentation of what is going on on the fingerboard. You don't have to be peering down over the guitar.

So you are resting the waist of the guitar on your left leg rather than on your right?

Yeah. It's very easy to see what's going on here. And very easy to get to.

Both ways work. Both ways are good. I really believe in a naturalistic approach to holding the guitar. Anything to me that looks like it's uncomfortable or a strain to the human body, that's a problem. The reason for that is, when you really love your instrument, you're playing a lot of hours. So you do not need something that's going to cramp up your shoulder...or your leg's going to go numb or something.

You want to be in a basic relaxed position. Your right hand position is critical. You want that right hand to be very relaxed where it breaks at the wrist. You are just kind of turning it around a little bit...and that's your playing position. Nice and relaxed, as it would fall normally. When that happens, your fingers sort of spread out a little bit over the strings.

Now a lot of guys play with their wrist straight and their fingers parallel to the strings. That's really bad, because you are getting tangled up in the right hand.

Proper hand position is good from just a physical point of view, number one; and number two, the generation of good tone comes from right hand technique.

You'll find that all good guitar players have in common a couple of good behaviors. One is this great principle called "economy of motion." There's not a lot of wasted motion going on ... you know, with the elbow and the arm moving. Watch any good guitarist, and they get there without a lot of external stuff happening. A rock guitarist may be dancing around the stage, but you watch him really closely and he's getting to those notes really well, in a smooth, economical fashion without his left arm flapping around like a bird.

All the good guitarists are like that. You have to get from point A to point B in a very short period of time and the only way to do that is to have no excess movement.

When that right hand is relaxed, your thumb is separated naturally from the index finger. And your index, middle, and ring are nicely separated also. And this angle of attack on the string happens to produce the best tone. You can get a very nice free stroke sound just by following through a little bit. Mostly it's the angle of attack.

Try to alternate fingers, that's important. If you're constantly banging on the same finger, often times you're not following through with your right hand, so you won't get a good tone. If you remember to alternate, then you get a better right hand follow-through.

You want to make sure when you're practicing that you are flowing through in a nice smooth arc. That follow-through is critical. I know it doesn't seem to make any sense...kind of like if you were learning how to paint, or something. You can't just stop, boom! in the middle; you have to finish the stroke. You have to go past the string in order to get that fluidity.

Make sure that your follow-through is coming all the way up to touch your palm.

Try to ingrain in your hand that feeling of that follow-through. Pretty soon you'll get a feeling of a flow going.

Tone is critical, it's a big part. In fact, that's one of the biggest mistakes many guitar players make; they don't seem to understand how important tone is... or maybe they just can't do it. How shall I put this? If you are making a rattle, or a buzz, or something that doesn't sound musical on the guitar, this is not good. You have to remember that your soul doesn't buzz, it doesn't squeek...doesn't crap out. It doesn't need these poor performance techniques.

Slack key is a finger picking style, and many guitarists are primarily flat pickers. In order to play this style should they learn to fingerpick?

It would be good for them. Honestly, this is a good opportunity to do this. Plectrum style certainly has its place in the world. It's a cool way to play the guitar, and sounds nice when guys do it. But it ain't the only way.

If you open up your technique a little bit, all the way around, it makes you a more valuable player.

It's not something that comes easy...developing the independence of your thumb and your fingers can be a challenge.

Nothing good comes easy. You can't take a pill and wake up the next day and develop a beautiful right hand technique. You've gotta work at it. You've got to be willing to go there to get the results. If you trust your teacher, that they're telling you the truth and they're not lying to you, and if you follow these techniques, then you will be there in a certain period of time. One thing that good teachers inspire is trust so the student can devote the time to getting there.

You often do a very rapid arpeggio that has almost the same effect as strumming, but it is just slightly finer.

Yeah, it's just a little more separated. I envision that as just my hand falling off the strings, from thumb down. It's almost like a harp technique. But that's just a stylistic thing. I think it's nice, because I like the feel of that. It's not all that difficult to do. You just sort of break off the strings with a smooth interval between each finger. Start very slow: brrr-ra-da-da, brr-ra-da-da... Then it just gets faster.

So maybe the way to practice that would be to grab a chord, and then slowly arpeggiate it.

Grab a four note chord; thumb, index, middle, ring; and slowly let your hand fall off in an even way so you get: bum-bum-bum-bum, bum-bum-bum-bum...

Ummm-hummmm....

Bum-bum-bum-bum, and then gradually build up to speed a little bit. So it becomes a little bit of a flourish: Bada-rump! Like that.

Yet on the page, that would just look like four notes played all at once. So that's up to the individual to interpret that.

The ornamentation is pretty neat with Hawaiian slack key guitar. For some reason these artifacts (if you want to call them) just sort of permeate the style. And the use of those little artifacts determine what kind of style this person has. That's how come you can sort of identify it, right? You hear a quick arpeggio and you go, "Whoa, that's Keola!" Or you hear an upward brush and you go, "Whoa, that's Ray!" These idiosyncrasies of everybody's style gives it some definition.

Because the way the modal tunings work, harmonics are fairly accessible. And they are usually in the melody somewhere, because of the open chordal structure.

So they're pretty friendly to use. And, of course they sound really great in the open tunings, they really sing.

Do you ever use false harmonics?

Yeah, once in a while. That's probably just me; that's pretty rare.

Vibrato seems to be a large part...

Left hand vibrato is very important. It's a lovely thing on the guitar any way you look at it; any style of guitar you want to talk about.

In that case you are just rolling on the ball of the finger, just starting out slowly and then moving rapidly as the note sort of.... Do you know what an envelope shape is? You have the attack, and the sustain, and then the decline....

Even in guitar soundboards, they all have their own envelope shape. Some guitars: Wham! they sound good, and then they have a second peak, if they're really good guitars.

Anyway, the point is, with vibrato, you start slow, and then build it up faster as the note trails off or decays. It sounds real nice when that happens.

Would you ever find actual string bends in this style?

Yeah, you do. Particularly in those little turnarounds; sometimes guys will stretch it and then go on to the next phrase.

What about all the slides in slack key? It almost makes the guitar sound like it's singing.

There are certain things that could possibly imitate vocal styles. That high Hawaiian falsetto stuff has a lot of slippery portamento elements to it. So that may have been a part of that.

Any time you make the guitar your friend, it teaches you these little tricks. Its cool to have this nice silky, sliding stuff and get up and stop where you're supposed to be. Kind of like riding right up to the fence and "Boom!" That's it; you're there.

This takes some time; at least practice half an hour a day. If you can't do that, then, why don't you just put this book in the bottom of your parrot cage, or something!

Buy it first.

Yeah, good idea.

What, exactly, is practice? Practice is having fun with the instrument in a structured way.

So the first fifteen minutes of that little half hour chunk of life that you need for the guitar may be technical exercises and just really firming up technique. Understanding just what these rudiments are. Muscular exercises, right?

Anything involving muscular skill means repetition. You've got to repeat these things in order for them to mean anything to your hands.

Do you suggest stringing your guitar with any particular kind of strings?

You don't want to use a real light gauge string....a medium gauge is probably the best for steel players. Too light and they're flopping all over the place.

For nylon players, use a good medium or high tension string. 'Cause you really are getting pretty slack with the low C.

I have a great electric guitar that I had custom made. You're not limited by the style of guitar...any kind of guitar will work fine.

In fact, I have a wonderful old slack key album that's all recorded on an electric.

Sure, an electric Gibson, or something.

Yeah, plugged... with an enormous sixty cycle hum going through the entire album!
Sublime music with this huge "Z-Z-Z-Z-Z-Z-Z-Z-Z-Z"!

I think that was that same studio I was at last weekend...

Ka Mua O Ka Mokuna

Section One

Getting Started

The Hawaiian slack key guitar takes as many forms as there are players. As Keola says, "This music is about you. When you play, you are revealing your soul."

Listen to musicians like Sonny Chillingworth and George Kuo play *Moana Chimes* and you may not even recognize it as the same song! But there are certain elements that show up again and again. By mastering these, you will be well on your way toward finding your own slack key.

Basically, slack key is a combination of a steady bass, played by the thumb, with an often highly ornamented melody line played on the upper strings. The guitar is tuned to an open tuning to take advantage of bass lines and interesting harmonic possibilities. Melodies may come from anywhere, though traditional Hawaiian songs from the late nineteenth through the mid-twentieth centuries make up the bulk of the repertoire.

Slack key players use every guitar trick in the book to make the music shine: slides, rapid slurs using hammer-ons and pull-offs, syncopation, chimes (harmonics), and harmonized melodies using thirds and sixths.

Taro Patch Tuning
D G D G B D

> *Every slack key guitar player that I know started with Taro Patch. 'Cause it's not too, you know, weird. It's sort of "user friendly" if you're a guitar player.*

Taro Patch, or open G tuning, is probably the most common slack key tuning. It already may be familiar to you in another guise: both blues and rock guitarists have used open G tunings for its wonderful combination of open strings, interesting chord inversions, and double stops.

Begin by lowering your first string from E to D. (Check your pitch against the B string, 3rd fret.) Then lower your fifth string to G, an octave below the 3rd string; and the sixth to D, an octave below the fourth string.

Strumming across all of the open strings in this tuning produces a G major chord.

As we said, slack key is a fingerpicking style of guitar playing with a alternating bass set against complex melodic lines played on the upper strings. In learning the songs in the next section, don't forget to give the bass its due. A wise old Hawaiian musician once said to Mark, "Yeah, bra', that's fancy guitar playing. But it's not slack key if I can't hear the bass."

If you are new to fingerpicking, or if you feel you may need a review, the following arrangement is designed to teach the basics. It's a very simple version of the nursery rhyme, *Are You Sleeping, Brother John?*, arranged to help you learn to play a melody with your fingers while maintaining a bass with your thumb. Feel free to skip over this exercise if you already know how to keep a steady thumb.

Bruddah John
Fingerpicking Excercise

Taro Patch

Traditional

In measures 1 and 2, the bass and melody notes fall on the same beats. Try alternating fingers for the melody. In the next two measures, notice that the final beat is played by the thumb alone.

Measures 5 and 6 introduce melody notes played between the thumb strokes. Finally, the last measures introduce a variation of the thumb pattern.

Practice *Bruddah John* until you can maintain a steady alternating bass throughout the piece.

The Hawaiian Turnaround

Many Hawaiian songs feature a particular two chord pattern that moves the song along back to the beginning. This vamp is so distinctive that steel guitarists named it *The Hawaiian Turnaround* and use it whenever they wish to give their playing an Island flavor.

Basically, it is simply a dominant seventh chord followed by a tonic:

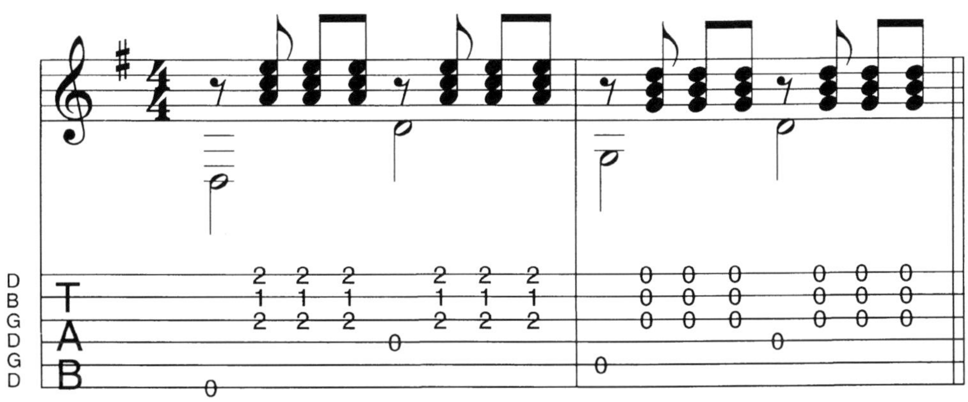

Each slack key player develops a personal set of turnarounds. Here are some variations. Notice the syncopation in this next example; play the downbeat with your thumb, followed by the A on the third string, second fret. Try to sound the hammer-on so the C falls on beat three. Finally, use your pinky to play the F♯ and G notes that end the run. The lick is easier if you play it out of this D7 chord position:

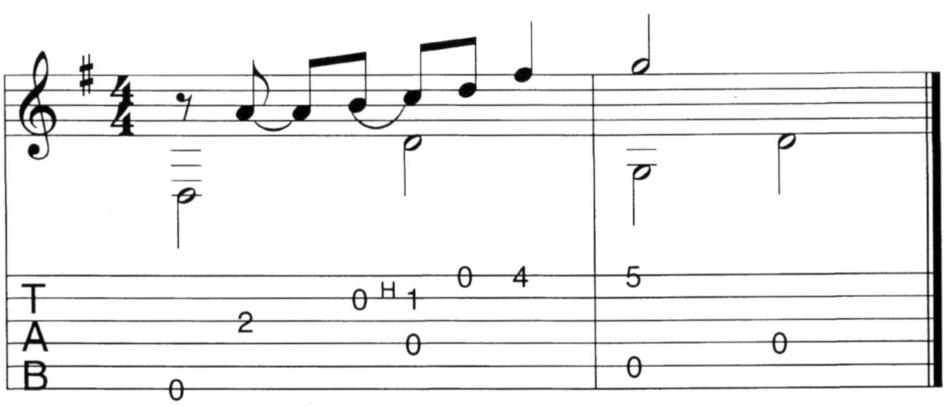

Notice how you slide into the final note in measure one just slightly ahead of the next downbeat in the following example:

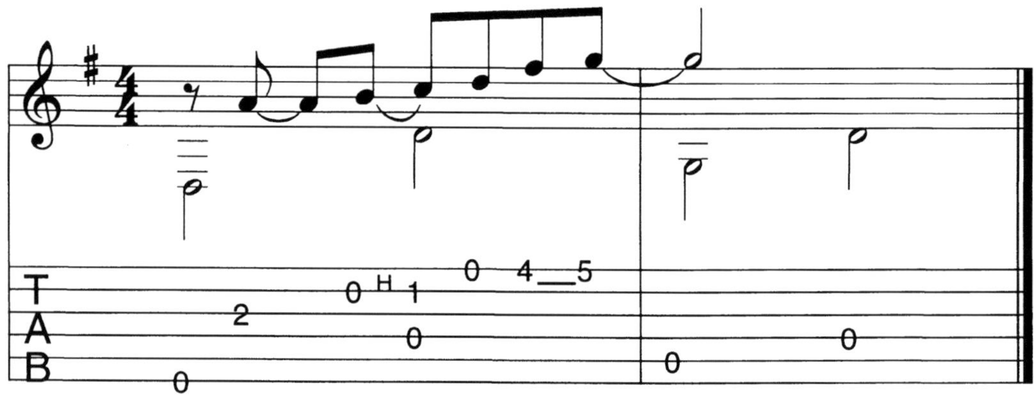

Now try the same thing with a quarter note pulse:

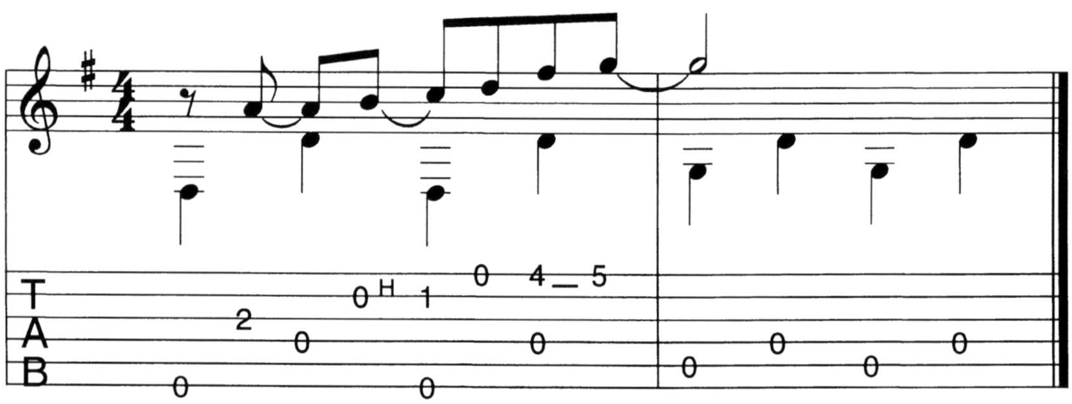

This next one is typical of the playing of slack key master Raymond Kāne. Play the low D with your thumb, then quickly brush upwards across the top three strings with your index finger; followed by an extremely rapid slur consisting of a hammer-on and pull-off. Just to make things more interesting, Ray does the slurs with an unusual upwards flick of his ring finger!

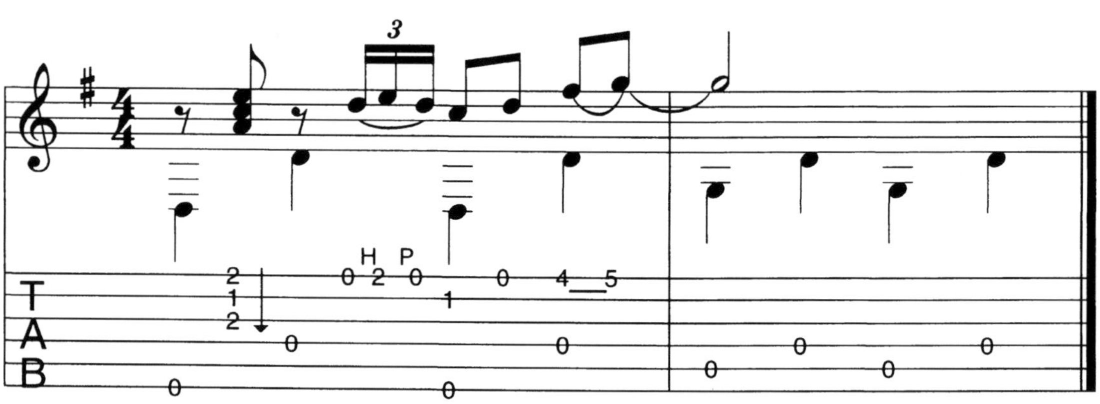

This lick is based on one of the defining characteristics of *Taro Patch* tuning, parallel sixth harmony played of the first and third strings. Keep your index finger on the third string and your ring finger on the first string all the time, and remember to let each note of the slide sound for its full value.

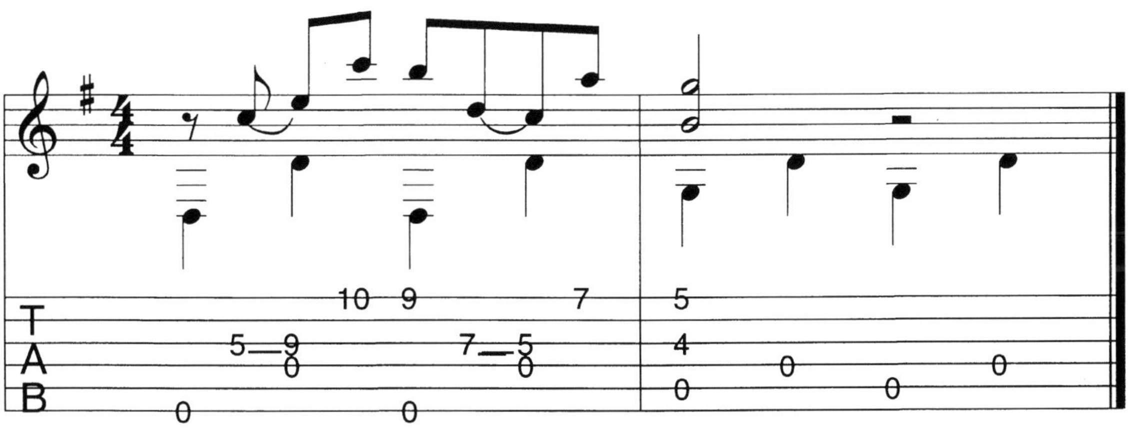

Practice stringing these turnarounds together in various combinations. You may even start finding some of your own. The example on the following page shows just how much music it's possible to get from a few simple elements. After you've played through it once or twice, begin adding some of the licks you've learned from the previous examples. Try to keep a steady, languid rhythm to your playing. You'll know you've got it right when everyone in the room starts to smile and sway to the music!

As you play through the tunes in *Taro Patch* tuning, you'll encounter several variations of these common turnarounds. A good way to begin developing your own personal style of slack key would be to substitute different variations for the ones in the arrangements.

Linked Turnarounds Example

Taro Patch

Taro Patch Tuning
D G D G B D

Kūwili

Taro Patch

Traditional

Kūwili

My mother, Nona Beamer, remembers her grandmother, Helen Desha Beamer, dancing this hula in the 1930's and being joined by ***her*** *mother, Isabella Kalili Desha. It seems to have been a spontaneous offering at family gatherings when my mother was a small child. It fell out of favor in the rushing tide of Americanism possibly due to the poetic disguise of sensual swaying and flashing eyes. Kūwili is a street in Iwilei, O'ahu, named for a fishpond and later the site of the old O'ahu Railway depot. The literal translation is "standing, swirling."*

Performance Notes

This very simple tune is an excellent introduction to the style. Remember to maintain a steady alternating bass with your thumb; this is the foundation upon which slack key guitar is built. No need to hurry, picture yourself lying in the shade on a black sand beach, with the tradewinds cooling your toes and you'll get the idea.

The pickup measure makes use of a chromatic run to lead into the downbeat of measure one. Play this run with your index finger.

Measure 1 Play the third string, ninth fret with your index finger and the note on the first string with your ring finger. This fingering is common to many *Taro Patch* tunes. Don't lift your index finger after sounding its note; try to let all of your strings ring as long as you can.

Keep this fingering throughout the measure:

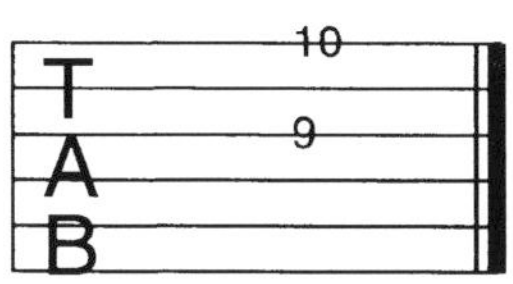

Measures 2–3 The double stop on beat one of each measure is played with the same fingers. Keep your index finger on the third string and your ring finger on the first string.

Use your middle finger to play the eighth note on the first string, eighth fret, and quickly hammer on back to the ninth fret.

Measure 4 Hold the double stop from the previous measure; there's no need to change hand position. This will help create the smooth, flowing feel that is so much a part of slack key guitar.

Play the note on the ninth fret on the first string with your baby finger; the pull-off may take a little practice. Be sure all three notes ring out with the same volume and tone.

Measures 6–7 This is the first ending of ***Kūwili***, when you reach the repeat sign, jump back to the beginning. Notice that the chromatic run in measure 7 is just like the intro, except that you have added a bass note.

Measures 8–9 Play this second ending after you have taken the repeat. For the final chord, brush downward across all six strings with your thumb, and let it ring.

Pu'u O Hulu

Taro Patch

Eliza Ha'aheo

Pu'u O Hulu

(The Hill of Hulu)

The lyrics of this song refer to the Wai'anae coast of the Island of O'ahu. Hawaiian music often reflects a strong sense of place, a love or longing for a particular area. Here, the warm rain of Mā'ili and the Kaiaulu wind paint a beautiful landscape.

Pu'u O Hulu is a prominent hill at Lualualei. The story says that Hulu, a chief, was in love with the beautiful Mā'ili'ili. Unfortunately, he was unable to tell her apart from her equally beautiful twin sister. To avoid trouble, a mo'o *(an* aumakua, *or guardian spirit) changed the sisters into mountains. To this day the lovestruck Hulu gazes with longing on the mountain that was once a woman.*

Performance Notes

Waltzes are a vibrant part of the slack key repertoire. The challenge for newcomers is to keep a steady alternating bass in a three/four pattern.

Measure 1 After the pickup, brush upwards across the top three strings with your index finger. Since this is a *Taro Patch* tune, maintain your basic fingering with your index finger on the third string and ring finger on the first string as much as possible, even when it isn't indicated on the Tablature. This will get you in the habit of playing with a comfortable hand position and set you up to begin improvising once you are familiar with the style.

Measures 5–6 Barre all six strings at the fifth fret with your index finger. Try to avoid clamping the barre with your middle finger; you may need it later! Use your ring finger for the note at the seventh fret on the second string.

Measure 10 No surprises; play this exactly like measure 1.

Measures 13–14 If you've been keeping the basic double stop fingering throughout the piece, these two measures will fall naturally under your fingers.

Pa'ahana

Taro Patch

Traditional,
attributed to James Kaholokula Sr.

Pa‘ahana
(Industrious)

A well-known story, song and hula reminiscent of a Hawaiian Cinderella story. The geographic area is Wahiawā, O‘ahu, where she lived in the hills, surviving on the food of the land, far from her ill-treating stepmother.

Performance Notes

Pickup measure Place your index finger on the third string at the fourth fret, pick the string, then slide your finger up to the fifth fret. Make sure each note has equal weight.

Measures 1 and 5 Move your index finger up the neck to the seventh fret—at the same time, reach up to the ninth fret on the first string with your ring finger. Don't remove your index finger after you've sounded its note; let it ring all the way through this measure.

Use your pinky to play the note on fret ten.

Measure 2 Remove your pinky for the first note, then move down to the seventh fret on the first string. After the second bass note, reach down to the fourth fret, first string with your index finger.

Notice that your bass pattern changes from the fifth and fourth strings to the sixth and fourth strings. You've changed chords from G to D7 and the open fifth string would sound out of place.

Measures 3 and 7 Play the note on the fifth fret, first string with your middle finger and leave it there while you reach up to the seventh fret with your pinky. On beat three, simply remove your pinky.

Measure 4 Play the open first string on beat one, then add your bass note on beat three.

The slide on beat four is identical to the pickup.

Measure 6 On the down beat, pluck both the first and third strings, then slide your hand down two frets. It may take a little practice to get the slide smooth. Otherwise, this measure is the same as measure 2. Good slack key players will often find ways to subtly vary the melody each time. After you become familiar with this tune, see if you can find a way to play measure 7 differently from measure 3.

Measure 9 The final chord is a G6, a sweet harmony often found in slack key music. Use your ring finger for the first string, your middle finger on the second string, and your index finger on the third string. Strum down all six strings with your thumb.

Lei 'Ohu

Taro Patch

George Akiu

Lei ʻOhu

This song is reflective of a "nationalistic" or "patriotic" genre that seemed to emerge following the overthrow of the Monarchy, and the annexation of Hawaiʻi to the United States of America. The form employs repetitive lines that often hele kaʻapuni *(to make a tour, go around, travel) a particular island or district (in this case the island chain) to promote a sense of ownership and identity. At civic clubs, church conferences and political rallies, people would stand up when their island or district was lauded, joining hands, they would sing at high volume with considerable enthusiasm.*

Performance Notes

Measures 1–2 Maintain a steady quarter note pulse with your thumb as you practice using alternating fingers to pluck the open strings.

Measure 3 Use your index finger for the second fret on the second string so you can smoothly reach up to the fifth fret with your pinky.

Measure 4 Move all the way into the ninth fret with your pinky just before you pick the downbeat. Add your index finger on the seventh fret, third string to complete the double stop. Since you'll need it for the next beat, place your middle finger on the second string (eighth fret) at the same time.

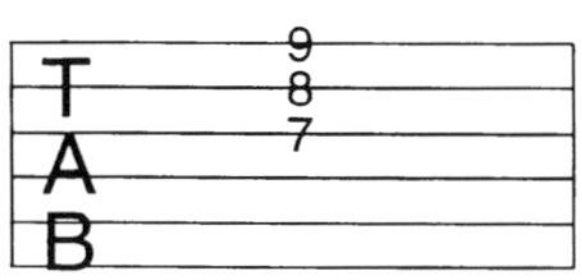

It's a good idea to get in the habit of looking ahead in the arrangements to see which fingers you will be needing. Using chord positions gives you that sweet music box sound so important to slack key guitar.

Measure 5 The first melody note is played out of the G major chord position held in the previous measure. Let the note ring as long as you can, on beat three release the chord and play the two open notes.

Even though these are the same pitch as the note you played at the seventh fret, using the open string gives you time to move your hand down the neck in anticipation of the next measure.

Measures 6–7 Notice the change in the bass pattern; these next few measures move to a D7 chord, so you can feature the two open D strings.

Place your index finger on the first fret, second string and your middle finger on the second fret, third string and keep them there for these two measures.

Measure 8 Play the bass note, then pick the open second string and hammer on with your index finger to the first fret. Timing your hammer-ons to coincide with the bass notes may take a little practice.

Finally, pick the open first string and move your hand up the neck to get ready for the next down beat.

Measure 9 Use your pinky and index fingers for the double stop; this lets you place your ring finger on the second string, seventh fret for the note on beat four.

Measure 10 If you haven't moved your fingers from the previous measure, you should be all ready. Simply pick the third string and you're there.

Measure 11 Like many Hawaiian songs, ***Lei 'Ohu*** incorporates a turnaround as part of the melody. Slack key players often use these last couple measures for embellishment and improvisation; we've included kind of a jazzy example that makes use of the dissonance in the first part of the melody.

The stream of eighth notes may look daunting at first, but there's not much to worry about. It may be useful to break the measure in half.

Begin by picking the open first string; hammer down with your middle finger, then pull off back to the open string. Finish beat two by playing the second fret, second string with your middle finger.

On beat three, play the second string, first fret with your index finger, then pick the open first string. Reach up to the fourth fret with your pinky, and finally slide it into the fifth fret.

Don't forget to put the bass notes where they belong!

Measure 12 This bar shouldn't pose any challenge.

To repeat the song, jump back to the pickup bar at beat four of this measure; or you can add one of the two bar turnarounds we've worked on as a vamp before starting over.

‘Alekoki

Taro Patch

Prince Lunalilo

‘Alekoki

This is a love song written by Prince Lunalilo, speaking of his lost love, Victoria Kamāmalu, sister of Lot Kamehameha and Liholiho. The storytelling quality of this song puts it in the category of "classic."

Performance Notes

Play this beautiful old love song with a great deal of feeling and a gentle heart. Don't take it too fast, 80 BPM is a good tempo.

Measure 3 Barre with your index finger at the fifth fret and use your middle finger for the seventh fret on the second string. This lets you stretch your pinky all the way up to the tenth fret. This is a lot easier if you are holding the guitar the way Keola suggests: rest the waist on your left knee with the neck slightly elevated and tilted back.

Let go of the barre when you move your pinky to frets twelve and fourteen. The bass note on beat four anticipates the chord change back to G.

Measures 5–6 A slight variation of the melody you played in the first two measures. Hold down your ring finger on the first string, your middle finger on the second and your index finger on the third string for the arpeggio in measure 6.

Measure 7 Place a partial barre on the first three strings with your index finger and pull off from your ring finger to the barre. Pick the next two notes and quickly remove the barre and move down the neck to play the hammer-on from the open second string with your index finger. Moving smoothly out of the barre to the open second string may take some practice, so take your time!

Play the notes on the first string with your ring finger to set you up for the next measure.

Measure 8 With your ring finger already in place, add your index finger on the second string, fourth fret. As you move up the neck, keep both fingers in contact with the strings.

Measure 9 This is the same turnaround as measure 7.

Final measure The last chord is a G6/9. Sweet, isn't it?

Hula O Makee

Taro Patch

Traditional,
attributed to John Kalapana

Hula O Makee

This is a romantic song. The Makee was a ship named after a rancher, James Makee. The ship Makee is symbolic of a sweetheart who has deserted her lover. The Makee goes aground on a reef at Kapa'a, Kaua'i, and is subsequently found by the ship Malulani, the hero of the story. Hawaiian poetry is resplendent with romantic symbolism.

Performance Notes

This arrangement is based partly on the playing style of Raymond Kāne. He plays and sings the song at a medium tempo with a subtle swing; take the piece at whatever speed suits your fancy.

Measures 1–2 Just a little turnaround to set things up. By now you should be pretty familiar with this; make the slide with your baby finger smooth and let the notes ring for their full value.

Measures 4–5 Play the hammer-on (measure 4, beat three) with your thumb. To set yourself up for measure 5, place the complete chord at the same time.

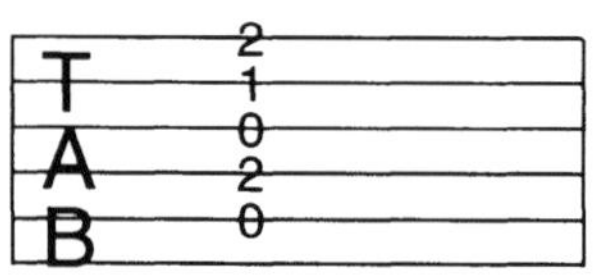

Play the slur (measure 5, after beat 2) as a rapid hammer-on with your ring finger from the open first string to the second fret followed by an equally rapid pull-off.

Measures 8–9 Once again, it pays to spend a moment looking ahead to figure out the best fingering. Notice that you will end up with a D7 chord by the last beat of measure 8, so use your index finger for the second string and your middle finger for the third string. This leaves your ring and baby fingers free to fret the first string.

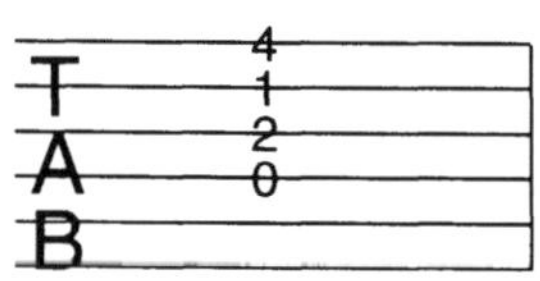

To set you up for the next measure, slide up to the seventh fret with your pinky and to the fifth fret, third string with your middle finger.

Measure 11 Play the double stop on beat one with your ring finger on the first string and your index finger on the third string. This is a quick hand position shift from the last note of the previous measure; make sure you can do it smoothly. Play the eighth note after beat two with your ring finger (first string, fifth fret), then slide that finger down to the fourth fret. Next play the second fret with your index finger and pull off to the open string.

Measures 12–13 This is the same turnaround you played for the intro on different strings. Try using your index and ring fingers for the notes on the third string. This sets you up to use your index finger on the second string, third fret. From there, it's easy to play the first string hammer-on with your middle and ring fingers.

Kāhuli Aku

Taro Patch

Winona K.D. Beamer

With Aloha

BV
rit.
Pau

Kāhuli Aku

*Passed down in the form of a chant by my great grandmother, Helen Desha Beamer. My mother, Nona Beamer, taught it to a group of young children in 1935, who were spooked by the chant. Mom added one note which took it from a minor to a major key and the children smiled. The song describes a friendship between the Hawaiian tree shells (*kāhuli*) and the Pacific Golden Plover (*kōlea*). In return for feeding the* kāhuli *shells, they promise to sing each night of the full moon, in grateful serenade to their friends the* kōlea *birds.*

Performance Notes

This is a wonderful little piece of music in *Taro Patch* tuning. The main idea here is to play in *nahenahe* style. *Nahenahe* in Hawaiian is the quality of music that is soothing, sweet, and satisfying. To play in this manner you must try to connect the notes to each other smoothly. For example, in the second beat of bar 2, play the 2nd string, 1st fret with your first finger, then add the note at the 1st string, 4th fret with your fourth finger. Do not let go of your first finger to sound the note with your fourth finger. Connect these two notes so there is no gap between them. Let them both ring.

Think about the *nahenahe* principle in your playing. Are you connecting the notes smoothly?

Measure 6 Place a barre at the fifth fret and hold it for one and a half beats, releasing the barre just ahead of beat three. Take it nice and slow so each note may sound for its complete value.

Measure 7 In this measure you change from a steady half note bass pattern to a slightly busier part. You will do this several times throughout the arrangement. How you use the bass is very important in slack key, and every player develops a personal style. Keola's use of bass notes is very free and expressive.

Measures 18–20 The song concludes with a pair of interesting vamps played as double stops. Gradually slow down as you reach the end, holding the last pair just long enough to let the music catch a breath before playing the final G add 9 chord.

Sase

Taro Patch

Solomon Hiram or Joseph Kokolia

Sase

Two composers have been given credit for this 1890s' song; J. Kokolia and Solomon Hiram. The lyrics are quite playful, describing the "sassy" girls of that era becoming adventurous and bold. This was the time of Honolulu's early influx of "Ladies of the Night."

Performance Notes

Play this song like the title, with a sassy kind of swing.

Measures 1–2 This turnaround features a little chromatic run; you'll use it a couple more times in the arrangement. Start with a hammer-on/pull-off combination on the first string using your middle finger.

Use the same finger for the second fret on the second string; then place your index finger on the first fret, second string and move your middle finger to the second fret, third string and brush upwards with your right hand index finger to sound the double stop. Finally, reach up to the fourth fret, first string with your pinky and slide into the fifth fret to complete the turnaround.

Measure 3 Note the syncopation, with the melody falling on the afterbeats of 1 and 2. This pattern crops up throughout the arrangement, so take some time to get it right. Like most *Taro Patch* arrangements, use your index finger on the third string and your ring finger on the first string.

Measure 4 Place your ring finger on the ninth fret, first string and your index finger on the seventh fret, third string for the first two double stops, then move everything down one fret on beat 2 1/2.

Slide back up for beat three; make sure the slide is audible. Next, move down a whole step to fret seven. At this point you can let go of the third string if you haven't already. Play the note on the fifth fret, first string with your index finger and pull off to the open string.

Measure 5 Form a complete barre with your index finger at the fifth fret. After sounding the downbeat with your thumb, brush upwards with your index finger. Use your middle finger for the notes on the seventh fret; it's usually a little stronger when it comes to pull-offs like the one on beat 4.

Measure 8 Make a complete barre at the seventh fret with your index finger and add your middle finger at the eighth fret, second string and your ring finger at the ninth fret, third string. Maintain this position for the entire measure. This is the same A9 chord you will play in ***Hilo March.***

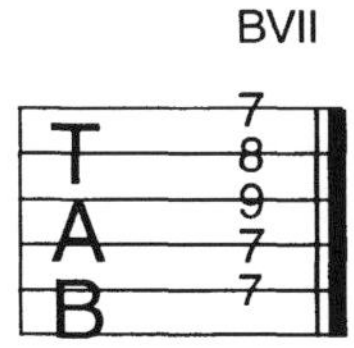

If you'd guessed that you use your pinky for the additional note up on the ninth fret, you'd be right.

Coda After repeating the turnaround, play the ascending chromatic run using your index finger on the third string and your ring finger on the first string. This is a fairly common ending; if you like it, commit it to memory and try to incorporate it into some of the other *Taro Patch* arrangements we've given you.

Hilo March

Taro Patch

Joseph K. ‘Ae‘a

13
1.

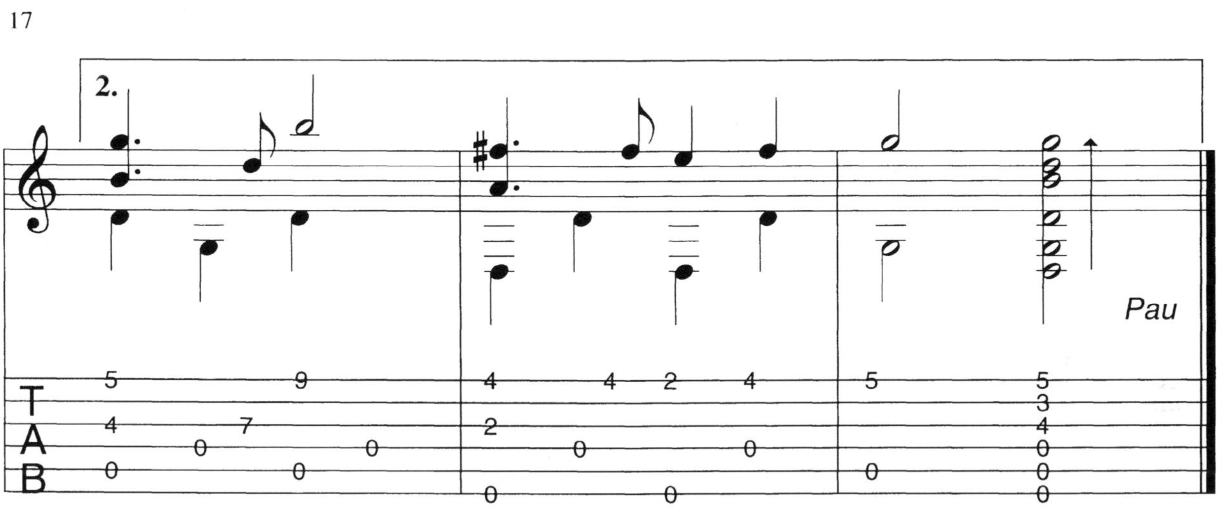
17
2.
Pau

Hilo March
(Ke ʻAla Tuberose)

Composed by Royal Hawaiian Band member Joseph ʻAeʻa as an official song for Princess Liliʻuokalani's visit to the little town of Hilo on the Big Island of Hawaiʻi in 1881. At the time, Hilo was endangered by a lava flow headed for the town. Prayers were offered and a celebration was held along with Henry Berger's arrangement of "Hilo March." The original title of this song was "Ke ʻala Tuberose" (The Fragrance of the Tuberose Flower). The lava flow stopped short of Hilo on August 9, 1881.

Performance Notes

This arrangement isn't too challenging, so try to play this standard with a strong marching beat.

Measure 1 Brush upwards with your index finger on beat one, then slide your ring finger down to the eighth fret and back again for the next two notes. Try to hold your finger position on the second and third strings to let the chord ring.

Measures 2 and 10 Play the double stop with your ring finger on the first string and your index finger on the third string. (This will get to be second nature after you've played in *Taro Patch* for a while.)

Reach back to the fourth fret, first string with your middle finger and then replace your ring finger for the final note.

Measures 3, 5 and 11 Barre across all the strings with your index finger at the fifth fret; use your middle finger for the notes on the seventh fret.

Measure 7 Play this measure from a partial A9 chord barred at the seventh fret:

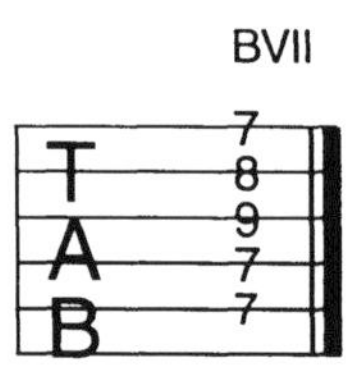

Using your index finger for the barre, place your ring finger on the third string, ninth fret and your middle finger on the second string at the eighth fret. Add your pinky on the first string, ninth fret.

Play the first double stop, then lift off your pinky and play the notes on the second and first strings, replacing your pinky for the final eighth note.

One of the secrets to great slack key tone is to play out of chord positions rather than moving your fingers for each and every note.

Measure 8 Quickly move from the full barre you held in the previous measure to a partial barre on the top three strings.

Measure 9 Place your ring finger on the first string at the ninth fret and your first finger on the third string, seventh fret. Play the first two quarter notes, then slide both fingers one fret down on beat three and back for the last beat.

Measures 13–14 Play these two measures with the same basic fingering: place your ring finger on the first string, your index finger on the third string and fret the fourth string with your middle finger. Listen to how the bass voicings change by playing a very simple descending pattern against a pedal tone on the low G string.

Once you are fairly comfortable with this arrangement, try your hand at finding another way to play the tune based on some of the tricks you've picked up by now. Add a few slides and slurs into the mix. Or vary the turnarounds in the last couple of measures. The choice is yours.

Hilo March has long been a staple of the Hawaiian band repertoire, with everybody taking hot breaks over the chord changes. Try to improvise around the chord positions, or make up a whole new melody that follows the general shape of the song. Listen to the CD for one idea of how to build a solo.

Maika'i Ka Makani O Kohala

Taro Patch

Traditional,
attributed to David Nape and Wm. Sheldon

Maika'i Ka Makani O Kohala

"Maika'i Ka Makani O Kohala" is the first line of this song and is still the title the song is known by today. Kohala, located at the northernmost tip of the Island of Hawai'i, is buffeted by many different types of winds. According to composer M.J. Sheldon, they are maika'i *winds—good winds. The figurative meaning makes the local people very proud to sing this song of love.*

Performance Notes

This arrangement makes extensive use of slurs and syncopation. It's not as difficult as it looks; take it slow until you feel comfortable. Sometimes translated as "Kohala's Fair Winds," this beautiful song is also known as *The Kohala March.*

Measures 2–3 Using your index finger on the third string, your middle finger on the second string and your ring finger on the first string, brush up with your right index finger on beat one to sound the chord. Then take a deep breath, you're going to need it.

Play the quick hammer-on at the end of measure 2 with your baby finger and immediately pull it off as you play the downbeat of measure three. On the next eighth note, remove both your ring and middle fingers and form a partial barre on the first three strings with your index finger. You're almost there!

Play the arpeggio, then reach up to the ninth fret and pick that note. Pull off back to the seventh fret as you reach the downbeat of the next measure. Remember to maintain your index finger at the seventh fret of the third string. In fact, unless you specifically need to move it, that's where it stays for practically the whole song.

Measure 5 At the second ending, move into the double stop at frets nine and ten and move back again to set up the second part of the song. By now you should be pretty familiar with which fingers to use.

Measure 6 Set your partial barre with your index finger again. Play the rapid slur with a hammer-on and pull-off combination using your ring finger.

Play the note on the eighth fret, second string with your middle finger.

Measure 7 When you reach this measure after the repeat you may wish to vary it a little bit. One idea would be to substitute a pull-off from the tenth to the ninth fret on the first string in place of the double stops on beat four.

Singing

The words are the center of Hawaiian songs. It's not really the melody, it's the poetry. If you have any relationship with the music you begin to discover that after a period of time.

There's the surface level of the lyrics, and then there is the kaona, *or deeper interpretation of the music which is often times the total antithesis, or the opposite of what the song seems to be about on the surface. It can be pretty complex psychological stuff. And lord knows we're a complex, psychological people. "Aaaaah, where's da food?!" (Laughs)*

There is also a participatory nature to Hawaiian music. You get a bunch of people together in a room.... and it's like, "Let me in. Let me sing with you." And Aunty wants to dance, and that 'ukulele, *that's gonna come out of the case! You're not gonna be sitting there playing solo guitar for too long in my family.*

Music is such a wonderful opportunity for us to share in our culture. For instance, in my family it just turns into a big semicircle, and everybody does something. Because it's just the way they are. And you learn things about Aunty So and So, and, wow, this uncle is pretty mischievous, I had no idea he had such a wild streak. All this great stuff sort of comes out of people.

Ka Lua O Ka Mokuna

Section Two

Two Approaches to Building a Slack Key Arrangement

Masters of the Hawaiian slack key guitar use their instruments to tell stories. One song may speak of the sweet sadness found in a lover's parting; another describes the beauty of a hidden waterfall, a third tells of a long ago shipwreck. Through skillful use of melody, accompaniment and adornment, each musician brings forth emotion from wood, strings, and aloha.

So far, we've been looking at developing technique and building a repertoire. Along the way we've suggested a few ideas you may incorporate to bring the music off of the page. By now, we hope you have tried swapping turnarounds from one arrangement to another, varying the melody with slides, harmonics and slurs, stringing similar songs together as a medley, and improvising a new melody based on the chord structure of the piece. That's a lot!

And we've only scratched the surface. These next arrangements illustrate two different ways to make your music come alive. The first states a simple theme, and then proceeds to build a set of ever more convoluted variations; the second introduces modulation for the first time.

Matt's Bounce is Mark's version of a common type of slack key guitar piece. The song is built around a simple ten measure form; as you play the piece notice how it builds in complexity and intensity. What started out very simply soon becomes a flying flurry of notes, slurs, and harmonics!

Listen to the great slack key players and you'll soon notice that they don't always stay in the same key for long. Modulation makes the song more interesting and keeps your listener's ears fresh. Particularly noticeable in Gabby Pahinui's ensemble playing, you can use this simple technique in your solo playing. Some tunings work better for this than others; *Taro Patch* is a natural. ***Keolaokalani*** is a lovely melody that moves easily from the key of G to C.

On Arranging

I envision it in my own work as rather being along a path, or, let's say, a hallway. A song might be an entrance somewhere along the way, like a door. You walk down the hallway, and you look at the light, and you look at how the thing sort of feels, then ask how can you become a part of that? If you can... I know this sounds pretty esoteric, but then that's OK. There are certain tools to unlock the door.

The first should be having some understanding of what the composer's intent was. If it's a love song, then you ought to know that this is a song about love and not a song about war. So you have to have some sort of initial understanding about what the composer is intending here, because that's important information.

The second thing is, now, how do you want to present that feeling? Some tunings are incredibly evocative and have a nice kind of palette or coloration, so you go into that room with that palette, maybe, and see what happens.

The beauty of the Hawaiian slack key guitar is that each tuning has its own coloration, its own texture. By matching the tuning to the song, or to what your interpretation of where the song is leading to, then you have some nice tools to begin work.

Your starting place is the melody of the song?

Yeah, I think that's pretty much true. It's real important to do stuff that musically really touches you because you never know how much time it's going to take to arrange it and you don't want something that's going to wear off pretty quick. (Laughs)

So for someone who is learning slack key, maybe a good starting place would be to learn the melody, learn someone's arrangement and then distill from that....

That's a very leading question, you're leading the witness.

I notice that you tend to arrange with modulations. Is that something that is particularly difficult in these tunings?

Yeah, modulation is difficult with open tunings, depending on the tuning.

But, as we get our ears more sophisticated we understand that if you play this one thing, droning along for five minutes, that may be a long period of time. So, just to create some coloration, some contrast, you can really do a lot by going some place else and coming back.

Every time you take that guitar and change those strings around, everything changes. It's a whole new reality, every tuning.

That's the most frustrating part about it. Because you're like being born again to the guitar. As a student, you've got to discover this stuff all over again.

Each player has such an individual style. You are instantly recognizable; I can hear Ray Kāne play and he's instantly recognizable, as well. You'll both be playing the same song, but it sounds entirely different.

That's why I believe it's such a special art form, there's room for all of us. My musical statement is worth no more or no less than somebody else's. You have this wonderful art form that is big enough for quite a few people to work with.

That's the way of it. You have a lot of different tunings you can choose from, and a lot of different interpretations.

How does one develop style? That's a little more difficult to describe. You sort of stumble around a little bit with the traditional forms and pretty soon you've got a path or something that's you coming out.

I think that my approach to guitar technique is to try and make the instrument as invisible as possible. To get to the music.... I would love it if I could just play in my head and still get the music across, because the whole idea is to try to connect with your self, and your soul and your heart.

As you know, the guitar can be a beast... you don't want to be wrestling with it in order to bring these feelings out. So you want to develop a relaxed technique so you can play for hours without falling down, or hurting your back. Or without carpal tunnel syndrome.

You want to be able to play in a smooth, connected fashion, without it being all chopped up, so you can have some opportunity to hear your own soul. It is a form of meditation.

How would you teach someone to take a melody and make it their own?

I don't know if you can teach those things. You can teach the rudiments of "here's how it goes." But I can't really pull the soul out of a human being...

That's why I always say, "You gotta play it from the heart." That's why in our arrangements we may put ***With Aloha.*** *You've gotta open yourself up a little bit. This music is about you. It's not about Mark Nelson, it's not about Keola Beamer; it's about* ***you,*** *the person holding the guitar.*

Now we can teach the rudiments; we can say, OK, there are elements that we use all the time: thirds, parallel sixths, these great little turnarounds, these wonderful tunings.

You've got to become comfortable with these elements as part of your repertoire. And then you will have some way to bring forth the music that's in your heart.

Matt's Bounce

Taro Patch

Mark Nelson

33
37
41
45
T
A
B
H P

Pau

Matt's Bounce

Early one morning, Mark met a popular Big Island guitarist to swap tunes. The man couldn't believe this mainland guy could possibly play slack key, so he asked to hear something. With the gentle murmur of the Kona surf for a backdrop, Mark played the most beautiful song he knew. Breaking into a huge grin, Bruddah Matt said: "Yeah, that's OK. But play sometin' fast!"

Performance Notes

Matt's Bounce is a set of themes and variations within a typical slack key ten bar structure: 4 bars of G, 2 bars of D, and a pair of two bar D to G turnarounds. (Sometimes this form shows up written as five bars of 4/4 instead. Either way, it's the same thing.) You'll find many, many examples of highly personal songs that follow this form, including *Whee Ha Swing* from Sonny Chillingworth, Ray Kāne's *Punahele*, and *'Opihi Moemoe*, Leonard Kwan's signature showstopper. Later, you'll see how Keola approaches this type of song with his original piece ***Ka Makani 'Olu'olu.***

In order to demonstrate some of the many variations slack key players use, we have included a fairly complete arrangement of this tune. It may look daunting at first; just remember that it can be broken down into easily digested pieces!

Measures 1–6 Play the harmonics by lightly placing your finger on the fret indicated. Notice that in the second measure of each pair (#2, 4 & 6) the final note is offset by a sixteenth.

Measures 7 and 9 Here are the turnarounds from the D7 back to the G chord. For these, and all similar measures, hold your index finger on the first fret, second string while you execute the rapid triplet slur with your middle finger; then slide your pinky into the 5th fret, first string just slightly ahead of the next downbeat. Practice these measures until you can do them in your sleep and the rest of the tune will be easy.

Notice how the tune is made up of similar phrases that repeat, often with slight variations, over and over again.

Measures 11 and 13 Rather than holding down the second string, fifth fret through the whole measure, play all the notes with your middle finger, jumping quickly between the strings. This gives the passage an indescribable lift and syncopation.

Measures 17–20 introduce a couple of variations to the basic turnaround that will show up again and again in several guises, so take your time to get it right.

Measures 21–24 Use your middle finger for all the notes at the fifth fret, slurs included; and your index finger for the F# at the fourth fret, first string.

Measures 25–26 Play this section with your index finger anchored at the first fret, second string. This frees your middle finger for the slurs off of the second fret and your pinky for those from the fourth fret.

Measures 27–28 Measure 27 starts out like the one previous; use the same fingers. Let go of your index finger after beat two, and continue up to the fifth fret with your pinky. Take advantage of the open string (the first note of the slur) to switch your hand position back to using your middle and index fingers.

Measure 29 Finger this the same as measure 27; but note that you slide into the fifth fret just ahead of the downbeat.

Once you've gotten the hang of linking the rapid pull-off/hammer-on slurs, begin concentrating on developing speed and accuracy. It doesn't have to burn; 103 beats per minute is fast enough.

Measures 31–40 You should be able to play this section with much the same fingering as the last ten measures. Remember to use the same finger for notes at the same fret on adjacent strings to give the tune lift: move your hand up and down the neck to place your middle finger in position for all of the slurs in measures 31–34.

Measures 41–44 Take advantage of the open strings to move smoothly up the neck, fingering the slurs with your middle finger and ending each time with your ring finger at the ninth fret and your middle finger on the eighth fret, second string.

Measures 45–46 This is a little tricky; play the first slur with your middle finger, landing on your index finger at the first fret, second string. Immediately shift your hand position to play the second slur (from the fourth fret) with your index finger, landing on your ring finger at fret five, second string. Another rapid position shift lets your play the slurs from the fifth fret with your index finger once again, landing at last (but only for a moment!) with your ring and middle fingers on the first and second strings at fret seven.

Measures 51–54 These measures are a variation of measures 41 - 44, with the addition of a slur from the seventh fret.

Measure 55 Barre the first three strings with your index finger and alternate between your ring and middle fingers for the rapid series of slurs. Finally release the barre and grab the harmonic with your pinky. Yes, it is difficult, so take your time.

Measures 65–66 Play the bass line with your thumb. After the last twenty measures, you deserve a break!

Measures 71–79 Pay attention to the notation to see which notes are sounded with your thumb and which with your fingers.

Measure 80 Sound the final harmonic with a rapid downward thumb brush. Congratulations!

As you can see, it is possible to build a fairly complex arrangement out of a few simple building blocks. By now you should have a pretty good idea of the form, so try mixing up measures or developing new variations. Mark never plays this song the same way twice, so you don't have to, either.

Keolaokalani

Taro Patch

With Aloha

Queen Liliʻuokalani

1.
2.
BV
BV
BV
T
A
B

BV
26
ritard
29
32
Pau

Keolaokalani

"No Keolaokalani a Ke'elikōlani" is the title of this song in my files. Although sometimes attributed to Princess Ruth Ke'elikōlani, modern day musicologists say it is actually a composition of Queen Lili'uokalani. It speaks mischievously of winking at "George." Was the Queen seeing a sweetheart? Maybe yes... maybe no.

Performance Notes

In this arrangement, the melody is first stated in the key of G major; after a short transitional section it is heard again in the new key of C major.

There isn't anything too difficult here; play it as sweetly as you can.

Measure 1 As always, be sure to look ahead to check for fingering. In this case you simply hold a chord shape and move it between two positions. Start with your index finger on the second string, third fret, your middle finger on the fifth string, fourth fret, and your ring finger on the fourth string, fourth fret. On beat three, move everything down two frets.

This basic fingering is found throughout this arrangement, so take some time to get used to it.

From time to time you'll need to pluck some notes on the forth string with your index finger; watch the direction of the stems for guidance.

Measure 5 After the initial chord, use your thumb and fingers for the arpeggio.

Measure 7 Here is yet another variation of a typical *Taro Patch* turnaround. Play this figure with your thumb.

Measure 13 The first ending brings you back to the top of the tune. Notice that the melody has been harmonized differently to create a bass line that walks up the scale.

Measure 17 Note the key change to C Major. The partial chord on beat one suggests a G13, acting as the dominant chord in the key of C.

Beginning on beat three of measure 18 the melody is restated in the key of C. Just to make things interesting, the melody is slightly reharmonized as well.

Measure 20 Now your turnaround is a G7 to C chord. Play the arpeggio with your thumb and fingers and "ghost" the E note by hammering back to the fourth string, second fret at the same time as the hammer-on to the second string, first fret.

Measure 27 The *fermata* on beat one tells you to hold this chord just a little longer, almost like a pause for breath.

Measures 30–33 Gradually slow down as you bring the song to a close, ending with a lush downward strum on the final C major chord.

Ke Kolu O Ka Mokuna
Section Three

No one really knows how many different guitar tunings are in use in Hawai'i; some estimates run into the hundreds. At one time, almost every family had a few private tunings that were never shared, only played for those quiet moments when the work was done and the household nodded toward sleep. Even today, each guitarist may keep a special tuning for just a single song. Nothing else will sound so sweet.

The next section presents a selection of songs arranged to show off some of the beautiful vitality of *kī hō'alu* tunings. As you encounter each new tuning, take some time to listen to what it says to you. Play through the music, certainly; but more than that, explore the sound of your guitar. Hear what each new arrangement of tones does to your understanding of the guitar. Where are your bass notes? How do you finger a basic chord? What would a turnaround sound like? Try to place a familiar melody on this new palette and see how it changes. Soon you will come to notice the similarity between different families of tunings. You don't have to start from scratch every time you retune your guitar.

One interesting characteristic of slack key tunings is their tonal flexibility. Depending on the mood, the instrument, or the range of a singer's voice, guitarists will take a selected tuning and move the pitches up or down, maintaining the same intervals between the strings, but varying the notes themselves. *Double Slack*, for instance, might be slacked down to F, or even all the way to A on a twelve string, and still retain its essential character.

Listen to each tuning. Hear what your guitar is saying to you. Take the time to explore this new world.

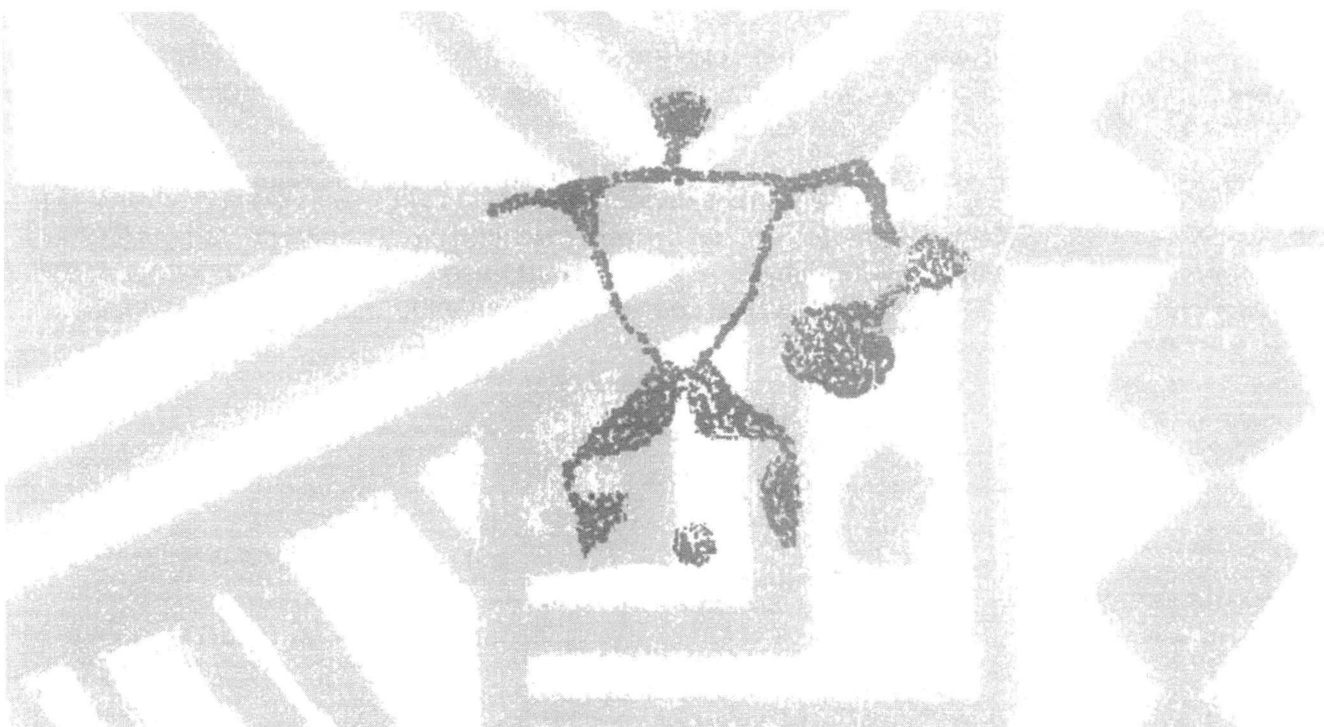

The Entire Instrument Sings

There's this beautiful stuff, sympathetic vibrations.... In a nutshell, that means we take that guitar and we pluck one string and the rest of them sing along. We're not touching them, we're not activating the string, we're not playing it. But the pressure of the air vibrating around the string generates movement so the entire instrument sings with each note.

Now that is magnified tremendously in these tunings that we use. It becomes a more active instrument because of the mathematical relationship of the actual chord, right?

So now you have this platform that is much more alive, and now the idea is you have to create order out of this chaos. That is what the Hawaiian slack key guitar is...that beautiful open sound. There's no sound really quite like it in the guitar world that I know of. You get a great modal tuning thing going and the melody notes have a sort of halo around them because of the sympathetic vibration. And the bass is beautifully supported with this undercurrent of strength in those low notes. So the melody instrument has a great deal of character and quality it didn't have before.

My guitars never, ever get tuned to "normal;" they don't sound good, you know? Because modal tunings are all they've worked in for twenty six years. They know how to vibrate. How to work. But you change them to "normal" tuning and they can't do it.

If you're gonna learn slack key, just leave it there, rather than yanking your guitar back and forth all the time. It's difficult to do...it's hard on the guitar. And it's very frustrating for the student to try and stay in tune. Just leave it there and see what happens. You'd be surprised how flexible, how comfortable you'll begin to feel about open tunings, to where you've forgot about the "real" way to play guitar.

C Wahine Tuning

C G D G B E

Taro Patch is only one of a huge family of tunings used in the Hawaiian slack key guitar. In the past, tunings were closely guarded family secrets. As you will come to learn, each tuning has its own character and coloration; sometimes simply moving a song to a different tuning is enough to completely change its mood.

Tunings that feature a major seventh are called *wahine* tunings (after the Hawaiian word for woman). Slack key guitarists make masterful use of the interval by hammering on from the major seventh back to the tonic; in fact, whole families of tunes have sprung up based on this simple movement.

Although not as common as *Taro Patch*, ***C Wahine*** has a lot going for it. Since the top four strings are tuned to the same pitches as in standard tuning, it retains a familiar feel for many guitarists. And the addition of the low C on the bass string lends a wonderful sonority to the tuning. Keola plays in this tuning extensively; so much so that it has come to be called *Keola's C*

From standard tuning, simply lower your fifth string from A to G, and drop the bass all the way down to C. Here are the pitches: C-G-D-G-B-E, low to high.

It may be a good idea to string your bottom string with a slightly heavier gauge string if you experience buzzing. Be sure to recheck your tunings often; the strings may retain some memory of their former pitches and go out of tune.

The first thing you'll notice about this tuning is that you don't have to relearn any fingerings for the top four strings. All the familiar scales and chords fall just where they used to. Of course, you'll have to take in consideration the two slacked strings when figuring out your bass notes.

The best way to get used to the feel of *C Wahine* tuning is to try your hand at a few turnarounds.

This first makes use of a typical hammer-on from the B note back to the C. This is a characteristic sound of *wahine* tunings, so make sure you practice it until it becomes second nature. Incidentally, this vamp is the foundation for the song ***Hi'ilawe***. Later on, you'll have a chance to play Keola's arrangement of this classic song.

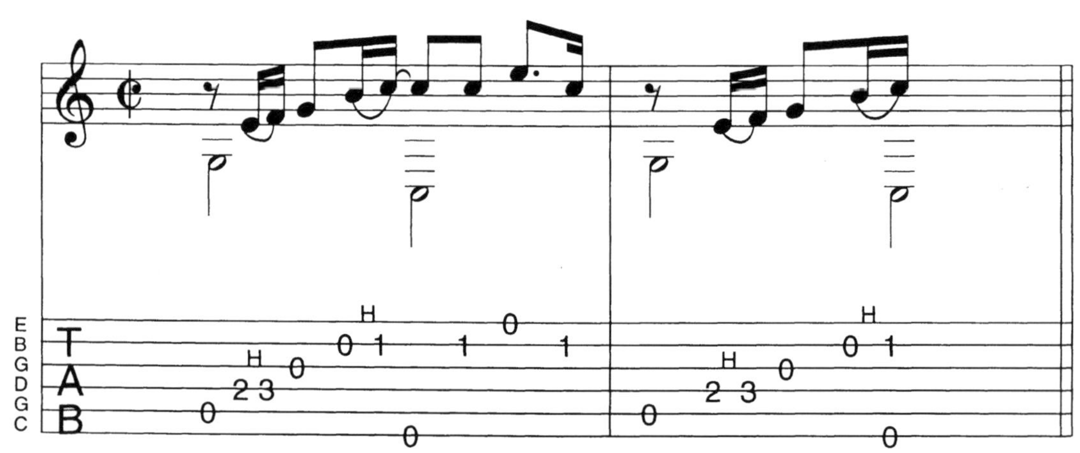

Keola makes frequent use of the open strings to bring a flowing tranquility to his playing. Here is a turnaround in his style. Even though the harmonic shape is the same as with the *Taro Patch* turnarounds you have played up to this point, notice how different this sounds—it's almost like water rippling down a moss covered rock.

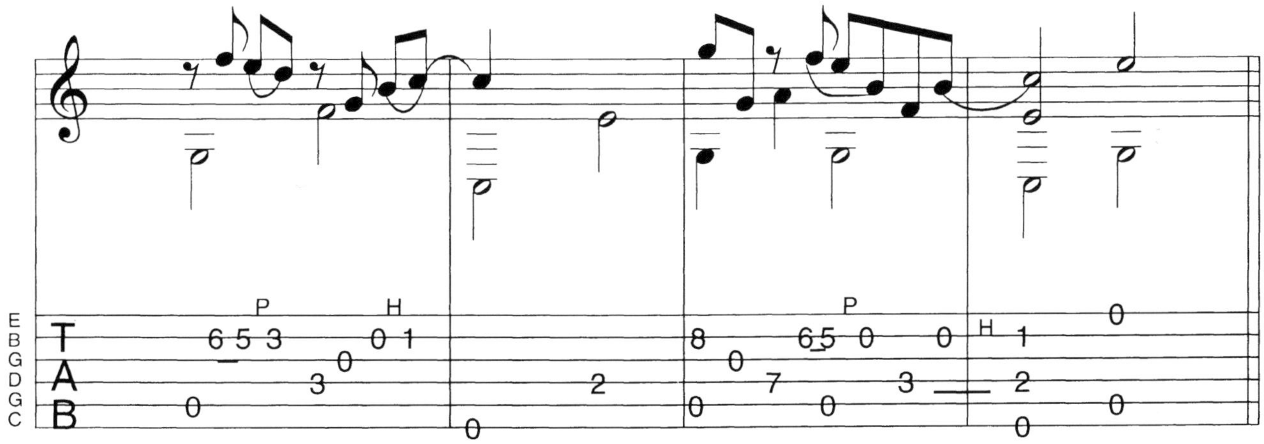

Play the descending series of eighth notes as evenly as possible, the pull-off may take some practice. The second half of the measure is an ascending figure played out of a G7 chord.

Notice how your thumb plays one of the melody notes in the first measure; you'll be doing this again in measure three. This gently flowing cascade of notes is characteristic of *C Wahine* tuning.

C Wahine has many beautiful harmonic possibilities; take a look at one more variation:

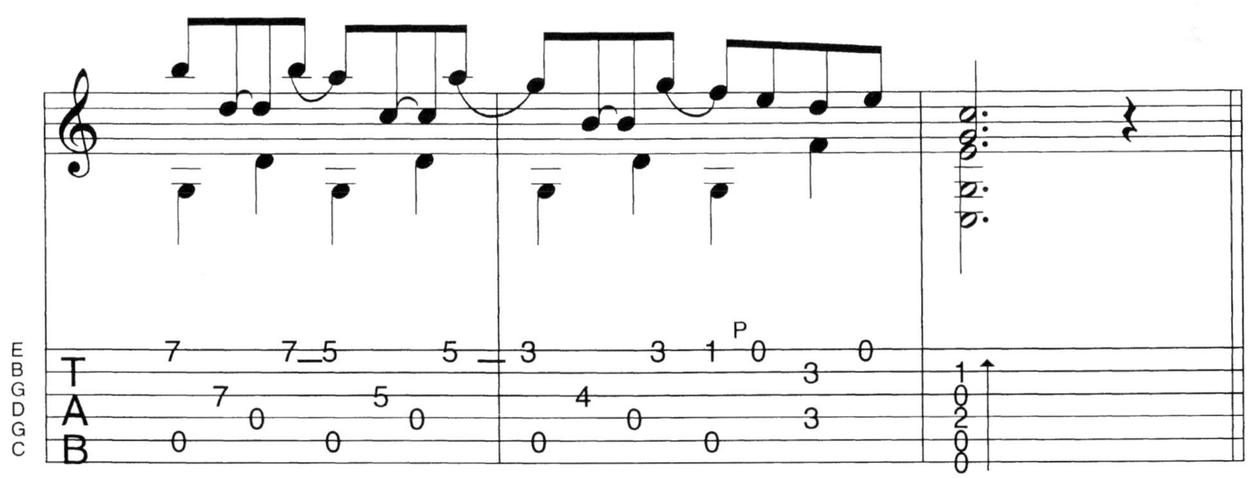

Remember to practice linking these various turnarounds to really get inside the tuning. And don't forget to create some examples of your own. As you play through the next few arrangements, listen for places where you can put your feelings into the music.

Ahi Wela

C Wahine

Lizzie Doirin and Mary Beckley

BV
BVII
Pau

Ahi Wela

(Hot Fire)

This song speaks of a burning love within and is a mele ho'oipoipo*—a personal song of love-making. The lyrics are filled with innuendo. Sometimes in Hawaiian music, we wonder if songs like this are appropriate for younger listeners. If it is crafted well enough, as this one is, it is not offensive. Love is love and the human heart seeks its expression in all forms of art.*

Performance Notes

As we have stated many times, slack key is a personal art. The guitarist may change the arrangement to suit the mood of the music, or the feeling in the air. Mark's recording of this beautiful waltz begins with harmonics on the open strings at the twelfth fret, followed by a descending series of notes similar to those in the examples we just studied. After playing through the melody, he adds another improvised figure as a bridge before repeating the song.

Think about how you would play the song to express your feelings as you study this basic arrangement. You might try adding your own introduction, or perhaps find a way to modulate into another key, such as F major. Once you are familiar with the melody and fingering on a new piece, you begin to tell your own story.

Measures 2–3 After the pickup notes, brush down across all of the strings with your thumb to sound a full chord. Try to separate the notes as a rapid arpeggio.

Take care with the long slide to the eighth fret in measure 2: be sure to give each note its due. Use your pinky for the slide and for the next note in measure 3.

Measure 5 Play the chord on beat one with your thumb and three fingers. Here's a good place to add one of Keola's trademark rolling arpeggios. Instead of sounding the chord as a single beat, play each note separately. The key is to quickly roll off the strings, starting with your thumb and continuing down to your ring finger. The whole figure shouldn't take more than one beat!

Measures 6, 8 and 9 Each of these measures begin with a downward thumb strum. Try for a balance between the strummed and picked notes.

Measures 11–12 Hold the chord after the initial strum, lifting and replacing your baby finger to play the single note passage.

On beat one of measure 12, hold your pinky in place while you move your ring and middle fingers up to the third fret on the second and fourth strings.

Measure 14 Let the second bass note ring as long as you can; then let go of the barre to play the eighth notes following beat two.

Measure 16 Now that you have played the final chord, how would you work your way back to the beginning?

Pūpū O 'Ewa

C Wahine

Traditional

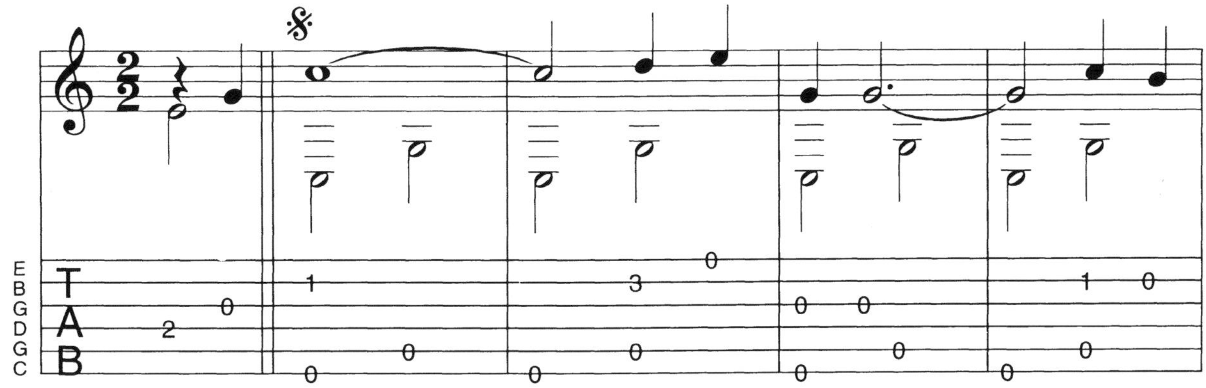

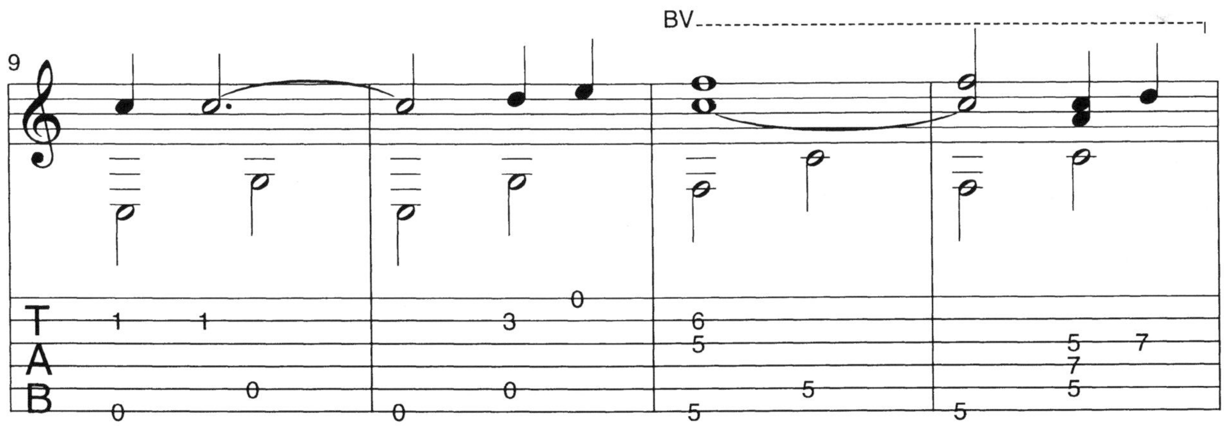

Pau
D.S. al Fine
BII

Pūpū O ʻEwa
(Shells of ʻEwa)

This is a very happy, uplifting, rousing, and joyous song. It honors the shark god of Pearl Harbor, Kaʻahupāhau, and mentions geographic features of the area. You might know this song as "Pearly Shells," a new set of lyrics by a popular songwriter for this favored melody.

Performance Notes

Pickup Measure Play the first melody note with your thumb; notice how the thumb never varies from a half note alternating pattern.

Measures 5–6 Everything is played out of a fifth position F chord:

BV

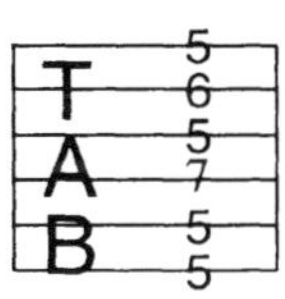

Measure 7 Brush upward with your index finger as you pluck the bass note. Or play it with a rapid downward arpeggio; the choice is yours.

Measure 15 This is the end of the A section; the structure is A-B-A. See the word *Pau*? This tells you where to end the song after you play the next part and repeat the A section.

Measures 16–24 The B section may be played with a slight swing to bring out the contrast between the parts.

Measure 23 This passage is played out of a D major chord:

BII

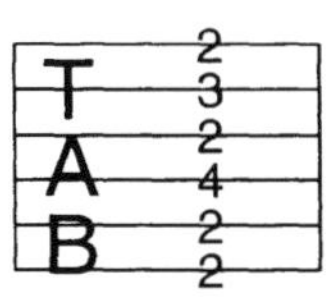

Use your pinky for the slide into the fifth fret.

Measure 24 The term *D.S. al Fine* tells you to return to the sign (at the second measure) and play down to measure 15. Remember, we use the Hawaiian word *Pau* instead of the Italian *fine*; both mean the same thing: Stop here, bra'!

Wehiwehi ‘Oe

C Wahine

With Aloha

Traditional,
attributed to Syvester Kalama

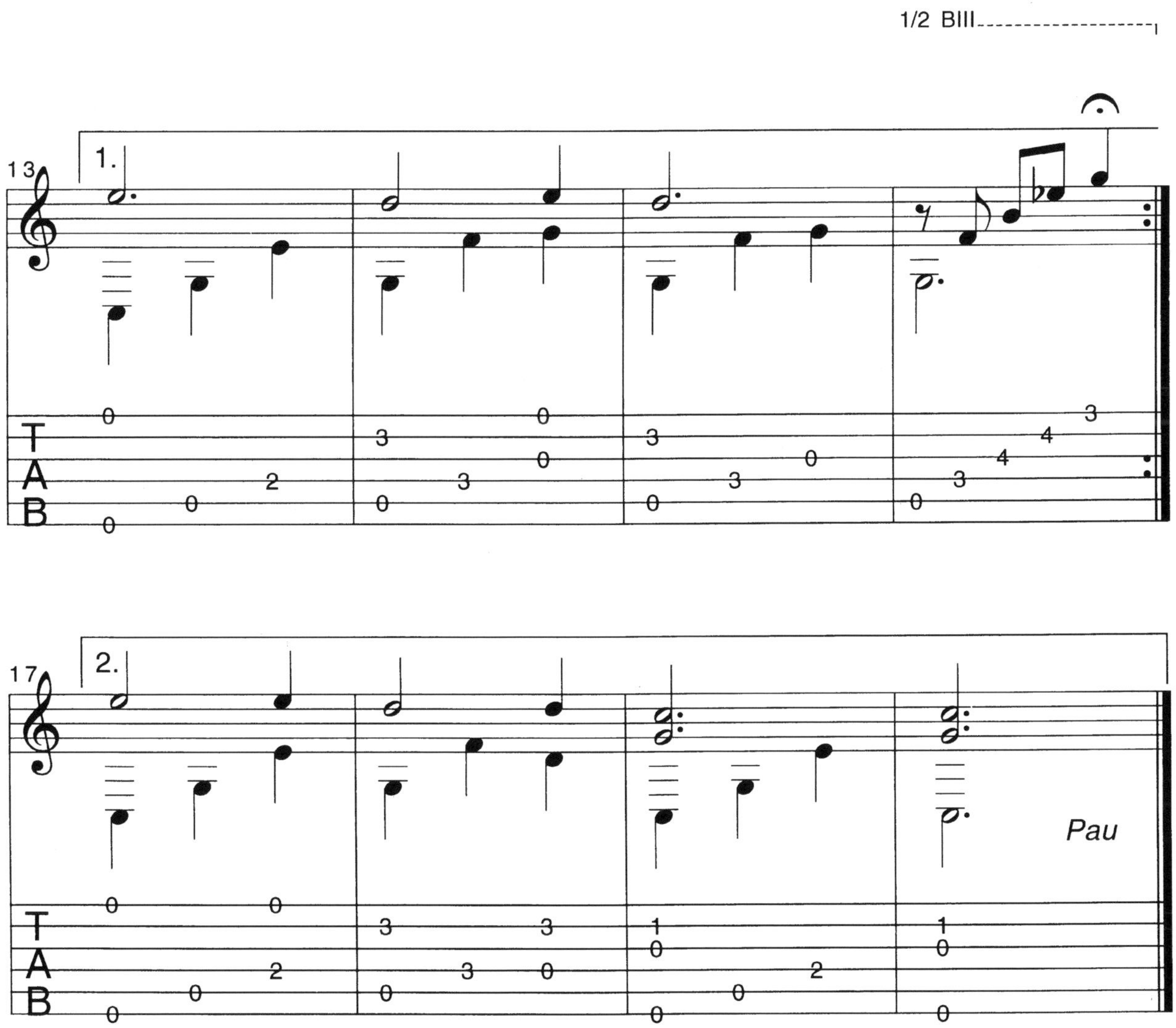
1/2 BIII
13
1.
17
2.
Pau

Wehiwehi ʻOe

Composer S. Kalama says "Thou Art Beautiful." Turn of the century poetry reflected the grace and charm of a bygone era, always alluding to romance in soft, sweet leo nahenahe *voices. The singer with this plaintive sound and expression captures a maiden's heart.*

Performance Notes

Measures 1–2 This arrangement uses a simple but effective thumb arpeggio pattern. Practice these two measures until the pattern becomes second nature.

Hold down a C chord for these two measures; use your pinky for the note on the third fret, second string on beat one of measure two.

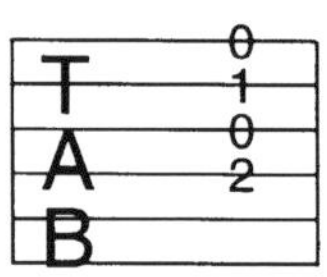

Measure 3 Move the thumb pattern one string higher for this and the next three measures.

For the G7 chord, use your index finger on the first fret, first string, your pinky on the second string, third fret, and your ring finger on the fourth string.

Measures 9–10 Hold a barre across all six strings with your index finger. These next two measures are played out of an F major chord; use your pinky for the high notes.

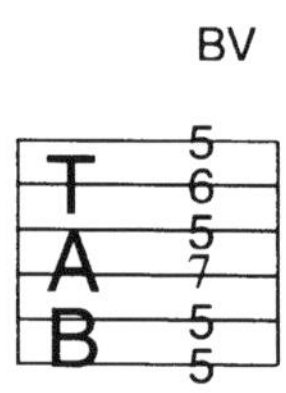

Measures 13–16 This is the first ending; at measure 16 return to measure 1 and begin again. The second time through the tune, skip the first ending and play measures 17–20.

Measure 16 The fermata symbol (𝄐) tells you to hold this note slightly longer than normal; think of it as a pause for breath before you move back to the beginning. The use of a G7 augmented chord reflects the jazz influences that crept into Hawaiian music during the Swing era.

Measure 18 The bass changes here to give the ending a sense of finality. It may be tricky to alter your picking after keeping the up same pattern for so long.

On the CD, Mark added an improvised introduction and bridge; you may wish to try something similar. Remember to listen to your feelings as you play and don't be shy about trying something new.

Modified C Wahine Tuning

C G D G B D

One way to look at this arrangement of strings is as a transitional tuning between *Taro Patch* and *C Wahine*. But don't be misled, it is a very versatile and common tuning. Sometimes called *Drop C,* this tuning is probably best known as *Leonard's C*, for slack key master Leonard Kwan. ***Modified C Wahine*** takes in some of the best features of both C and G tunings. It's easy to get to from either, and, if you are used to *Taro Patch*, you don't have to totally relearn the fingerboard.

From *Taro Patch*, simply slack your bass string down another whole step, from D to C.

From *C Wahine*, lower the first string from E to D.

And, from standard tuning, slack your first string from E to D; lower the fifth a whole step to G, and slack the bass string all the way down to C.

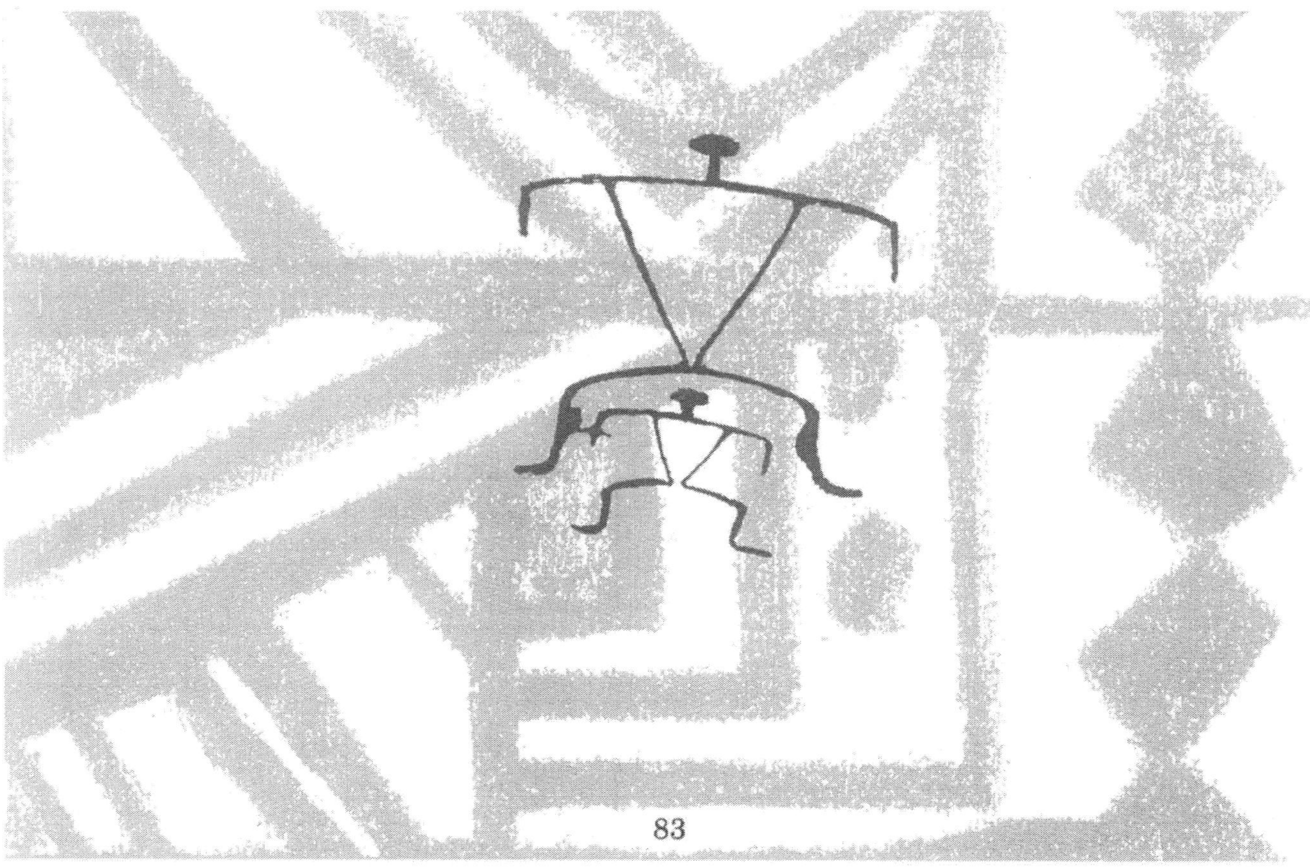

'Ulili E

Modified C Wahine

Traditional

ʻŪlili Ē
(Wandering Tattler)

This bird is a regular winter migrant to Hawaiʻi and is the subject of this nature song. Its bird call is the basis of a generic name for any type of whistle made of bamboo that when blown, sounds like the bird. The curious behavior of the bird is likened to human characteristics.

The words of this song describe the antics of a sandpiper skittering back and forth as the waves lap along the shore. A fragment of an old song, it may have been composed by Bina Mossman. It is often difficult to determine exactly who actually wrote an individual song, since in the old days the Hawaiians would pass along new songs by word of mouth with a rapidity that astonished the missionaries.

Performance Notes

The only tricky part of this arrangement is the rhythm of the double stops in the first four measures. Like many older Hawaiian songs, it really doesn't sit on the page well, no matter how you try to notate it.

The best way to get the feel for the rhythm is to ignore the bar lines altogether and simply listen to Keola's recording on the CD.

Measures 1–4 Pluck all the double stops with two fingers, rather than playing them as brushes. Don't forget that measure 4 only gets two beats.

Measures 6, 10, and 14 Move your picking hand back towards the bridge slightly when you sound the harmonics. Subtle shifts like this can add a great deal of coloration to your playing.

Measure 16 Keola slows this measure slightly to bring the piece to a restful conclusion. Play the final harmonics as double stops and let them ring.

Mauna Loa Tuning

D G D D G D

This family of tunings features an interval of a fifth between the top two strings; slides and sweet harmonies are characteristic. Like *Taro Patch*, ***Mauna Loa*** makes extensive use of double stops. You'll notice that many of the fingerings are vaguely familiar from your experience with *Taro Patch* tuning. However, rather than maintaining fingers on the first and third strings, you finger the first and second strings, brushing upwards to sound the third string as a drone.

To tune to *Mauna Loa* from *Taro Patch*, simply slack the second string until it is the same pitch as the open third string, then drop the third string down to match the fourth: D-G-D-D-G-D, low to high.

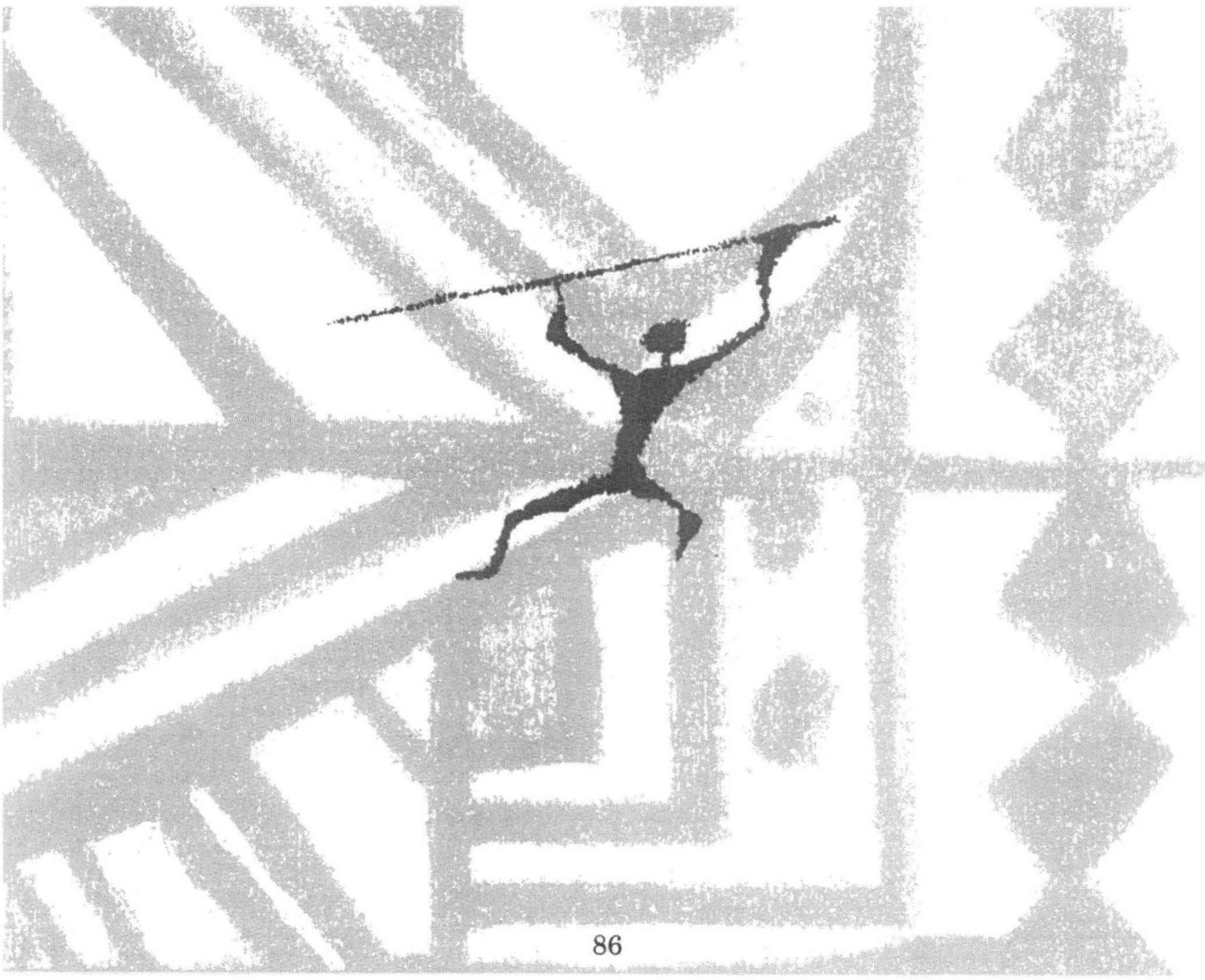

Kī Hōʻalu

Mauna Loa

Traditional

18
22
26
Pau

Kī Hōʻalu

No tune captures the indescribable essence of Hawaiian guitar playing better than this lovely piece. Like many slack key standards, there are probably as many ways to play this traditional tune as there are grains of sand on the beach at Waikīkī; the one quality they all have can only be described by the word nahenahe*—a certain sweet lilt that perfectly fits the feeling of moonlight reflecting on the surface of a calm tropical ocean.*

Performance Notes

This arrangement is based somewhat loosely on the playing of slack key master Leonard Kwan. He has recorded it twice: once in the key of A (E A E E A E) and more recently in a variation of G **Mauna Loa** tuning (D G D E G D).

Don't take this too fast—a tempo of around 80 BPM is plenty quick.

Measures 1–5 Set the mood of the piece with a set of upward strums. Although it isn't notated, extend the brush upward to include the third string on measures 1 and 3. Generally, you may include the open third string whenever it sounds good; use your ears and your taste to determine where that is. (For the sake of clarity, we've only notated the brushes in the first five measures.)

Measures 6–15 Sound familiar? Basically, the tune ***Kī Hōʻalu*** is a set of variations within the ten bar form you studied earlier in the book. The structure gives you a great deal of room to improvise, so study it carefully.

There isn't anything here you haven't seen before. Play the piece with a gentle lilt and be sure the slides are smooth and last their full length.

Beginning at measure 16, we've given you one variation on the basic theme. Notice how just a few simple alterations can keep the music interesting.

When you are familiar with the tuning, try to substitute your own variations.

Measures 26–27 Another two bar turnaround. At this point, you may choose to stop, return to the beginning and play everything again, or repeat from measure 6 and add your own variations. It's totally up to you.

C Major Tuning

C G E G C E

Not every *kī hō'alu* tuning slacks the strings; sometimes you have to raise a couple. Here is an unusually beautiful tuning made up of two C major triads; listen to how the strings vibrate in sympathy with each note and double stop! Atta Isaacs, the great slack key player who worked extensively with Gabby Pahinui, used this tuning with such beautiful effect it's sometimes called *Atta's C.*

From standard tuning, raise your second string one half step to C. Next, raise the fourth string from D to E, and slack the fifth string from A down a full step to G. Finally, slack your bass all the way down to C. Strumming across all of the strings produces a pair of C major chords.

Another way to get into this tuning is from *C Wahine*: from there, simply raise your second and fourth strings to the desired pitches.

You may run across this tuning slacked down to the key of B flat, another example of how flexible *kī hō'alu* tunings can be.

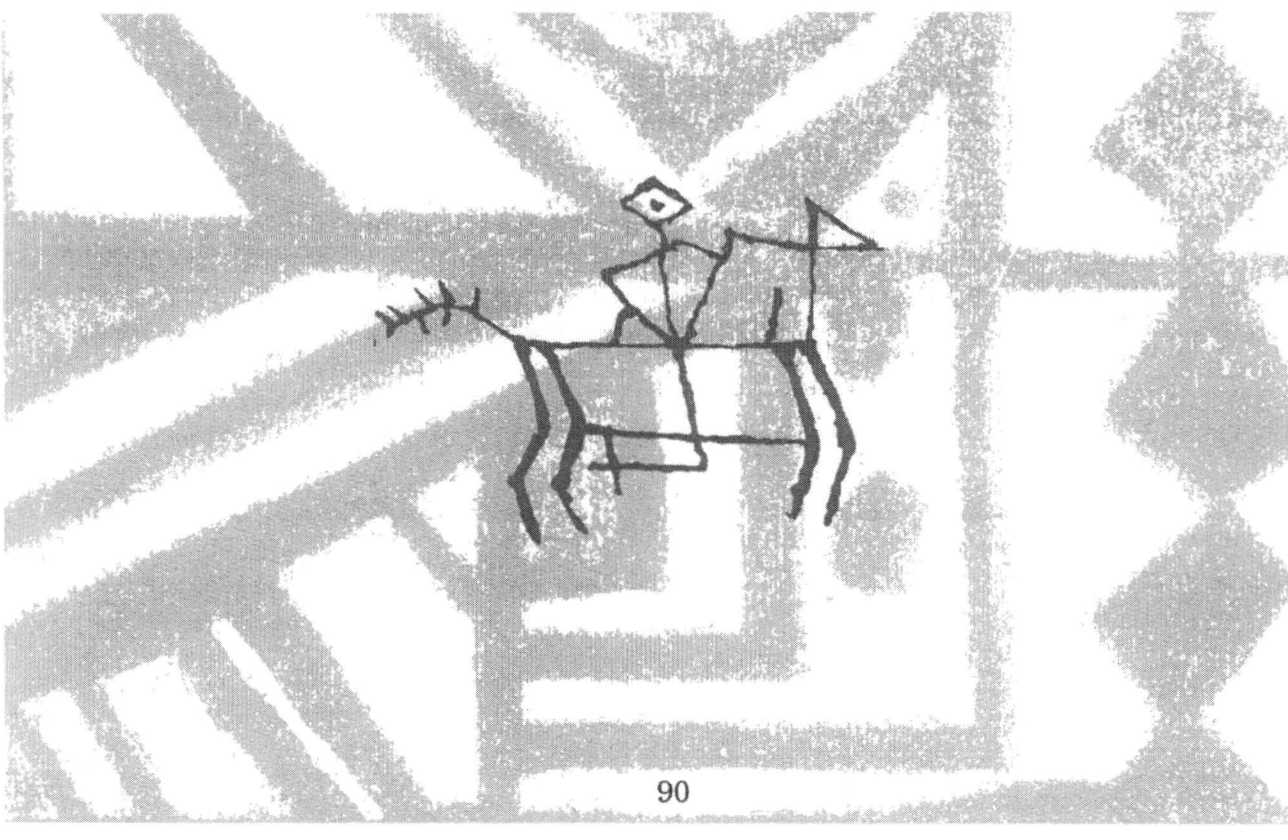

Sweet Leilehua

C major tuning

King Kalākaua

Sweet Leilehua

His majesty, King David La'amea Kalākaua, is the composer of this song written in a popular style of the mid 1800s—that of using English words intermittently.

The lehua *tree bears a beautiful red flower that blooms in great profusion on the Island of Hawai'i.*

Performance Notes

Aside from the use of an unfamiliar tuning, the arrangement itself is fairly simple. Although it keeps a steady quarter note pattern, your thumb gets a bit of a workout moving between the bottom four strings.

Remember to play with a great depth of feeling and let your aloha flow.

Measures 1–2 These two measures act as an introduction, or use them as a turnaround to keep the music going. Use your pinky for the slide from the fourth to the fifth fret.

Measure 4 For this song you will be playing many notes on the third string with your thumb, but the basic quarter note alternating pattern remains constant. Be sure to check the notation for help with fingering.

Measure 5 Pick the top note (first string, fifth fret) as you complete the slide begun in the previous measure.

Measure 6 Use your middle finger for the long slide from the fifth to the ninth fret.

Measures 9–10 It may look complicated, but simply place a partial barre across the first four strings and ascend up the neck.

Measures 11–12 Like the two bar introduction, this section may also function as an interlude between repeats. For a coda, gradually slow down; then play the final chimes as a downstroke with your thumb.

D Wahine Tuning

D A D F♯ A C♯

As we've said, *wahine* tunings always contain a major seventh interval; in ***D Wahine*** changing from the tonic to the dominant chord and back again requires moving just one finger! Talk about a relaxed approach to the guitar.

To tune to *D Wahine* you need to adjust almost every string on your guitar.

There are a couple of ways to get into this tuning. From standard tuning, slack your bass string to D, an octave below the fourth string. Next, slack the second string from B to A. The third string moves down one half step to F♯; check your tuning against the fourth string fretted at the fourth fret. Finally, drop your first string one half step to C♯. Press down the first string at the first fret and strum across all of the strings to check your tuning, you should hear a D major chord.

Then fret the third string at the first fret and listen to the sound of the A dominant seventh chord. (Technically, it's an A11 because of the open D string. Pretty jazzy.) Practice moving back and forth between these two simple fingerings to get the feeling of *D Wahine*.

Hame Pila

D Wahine

Traditional,
attributed to Charles Ka'apā

Hame Pila

No one in my family knows much about this old song. Kaliko thought the title might be a play on somebody's name, sort of a private joke. It is most likely a hula ku'i. Ku'i *means to join, splice, unite. The concept of joined hula is an interpretive dance that unites the old traditional steps with new steps. This form arose during the days of King Kalākaua—Hawaii's Merry Monarch. The lyrics are what we call* kolohe—*mischievous. This style of writing lyrics (very* kolohe*) was notably popular about three generations ago.*

Performance Notes

This simple little tune is a good introduction to ***D Wahine*** tuning. Like all *wahine* tunings, you need to hold down at least one note to sound the tonic chord. In this case, put your index finger on the first string at the first fret for a D major chord.

Measure 3 Hold down the fourth string at the second fret with your middle finger for the whole measure. Use your pinky for the first string, third fret and pull off to your index finger at the first fret.

After sounding the open first string, use your ring finger for the second string, second fret. Continue down the scale, using your index finger on the third string, first fret. After the final bass note, reach up with one of your right hand fingers to play the melody note on the fourth string.

Measure 5 The rapid hammer-on figures after the bass notes are typical of arrangements in this tuning. Play them using your index finger.

Isalei

D Wahine

Traditional Fijian

To Coda
D.S. al Coda
Coda
ritard

Isalei

This is a traditional Fijian song. In Polynesia, it is common to share songs and melodies. Beautiful melodies spread with the tradewinds from one island to the next. The song depicts a love for Fiji and a longing to return. Mark learned this lovely version from a friend now living in California whose aunt used to sing her to sleep many years ago.

Performance Notes

Measure 1 After the hammer-on in the pickup measure, simply walk up the scale. You may add a hammer-on from the open first string to the first fret and a slide into the fifth fret (measure 2) to give the tune a little more character.

Measure 6 Hold down the second string at the second fret with your ring finger and the fifth string at the same fret with your middle finger. Maintain this position for the entire measure.

Measure 10 Use the same fingering as measure 6, with the addition of your index finger on the third string, first fret to complete the G major chord.

Measures 12–13 At the phrase *D.S. al Coda*, return to the first measure, where you see the sign (𝄋), and play all the way down through measure 12. When you see the phrase *To Coda*, jump to measure 14.

Rather than merely repeating the arrangement, try to find your own variations using slides, slurs and double-stops.

Measure 14 The coda begins here; gradually slow the tempo slightly to bring the song to a close.

How Keola Almost Missed Lunch

When you are a student, one of the best ways to learn is by imitation. You find someone whose work you admire, and then you emulate them. You'd sit at their feet and maybe, you know, bring some fish, or taro or something... Fish works really good! ... and make yourself useful. I mean, you didn't sit there and ask questions and say "Hey, help me out here; I'm trying to do this, I'm trying to figure this out." None of that ever worked.

And then, when you have a basic understanding of the structure of the thing, then there is room for you to put in your own thoughts, your own feelings or interpretation.

And that's how most of us got to learn.

For me, the earliest influence was Aunty Alice Nāmakelua, who was kind of my mentor. She had these beautiful little scale-like patterns that would fit around the song. And those scale patterns would continue under the lyrics of the song. She would play **Hi‘ilawe** *or something like that, and it would have that lovely little pattern in it. She'd play another song and it would have kind of the same pattern in it.*

Now when she heard guys like Ray Kāne and Gabby Pahinui, she thought they were kind of radical. The reason was that's not the way she heard slack key. That's not the way she was taught. Her brother was the one that taught her, they were cowboys. And the way Gabby and those guys played had nothing to do with her style of slack key. Her style was really very different, more of a counterpoint.

She was eighty six years old.

Here's a story: When I was a teenager, sixteen years old, I'd drive to her house and take her out to lunch. I didn't have a very nice car, it was like a really beat-up sports car. You know...dented doors and the muffler dragging along the ground, and a big coat-hanger antenna and the seats were all torn up. This thing was a piece of junk.

So I go to her house and a knock on the door and I say "Aunty Alice, I'm here to take you to lunch." She comes out and she has this beautiful mu‘umu‘u *on and these black lace gloves and a beautiful hat...and she just looks like a million bucks!*

So I'm walking over and she's getting closer to the car....and she's looking at me...and she says, in Hawaiian, "What is this?"

And I go, "This is my car."

She says, "Come back when you've got a better car!"

My mother thought that was so funny till I went and borrowed her car.

B♭ Wahine Tuning

F B♭ C F A D

Keola's mentor, Aunty Alice Nāmakelua, taught him this unusual tuning in the key of B♭. Unlike most of the tunings we've explored so far, you must raise the pitch on a pair of strings, while lowering others.

From standard tuning, begin by lowering each of your top four strings a full tone. Next, raise the fifth string one half step, to B♭, and raise the bottom string to F. Hold a chord with your index finger on the second string, first fret, and your ring finger on the fourth string, second fret to check your tuning.

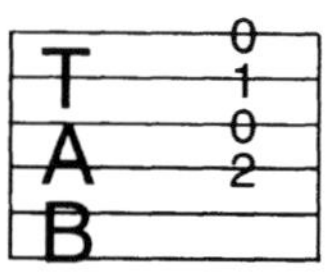

This tuning shares many similarities with *C Wahine*; in fact, save for the fact that the relationship of your two bass strings are reversed, with the tonic now on the fifth string, fingerings for both tunings are identical.

As Keola mentions, Aunty Alice Nāmakelua played an intricate series of ascending and descending figures as accompaniment to her singing. The following example will give you a taste of an almost forgotten world.

Aunty Alice Nāmakelua Slack Key

Bb Wahine

Traditional

F Wahine Tuning
C F C G C E

The next arrangement uses a beautiful tuning in the key of F. This is another tuning Keola uses extensively; like *C Wahine* it lowers the bass string all the way down to C. Listen to the way your guitar sings with those glorious low notes! You may find that you need to use heavier gauge strings on your two lowest strings to get a pure, ringing tone.

From standard tuning, raise your second string one half step from B to C; check the pitch against the third string at the fifth fret. Next, drop the fourth string a whole step to C. You can compare its pitch to that of the fifth string at the third fret.

At this point, it's easy to take the bass string all the way down from E to C. It will sound one octave lower than the open fourth string. Finally, lower the fifth string from A to F. It's quite a drop; check its pitch against the bass string fretted at the fifth fret.

You may notice similarities in fingerings between *C Wahine, B♭ Wahine*, and ***F Wahine*** tunings; in fact, it is not too difficult to transpose an arrangement from one to the other.

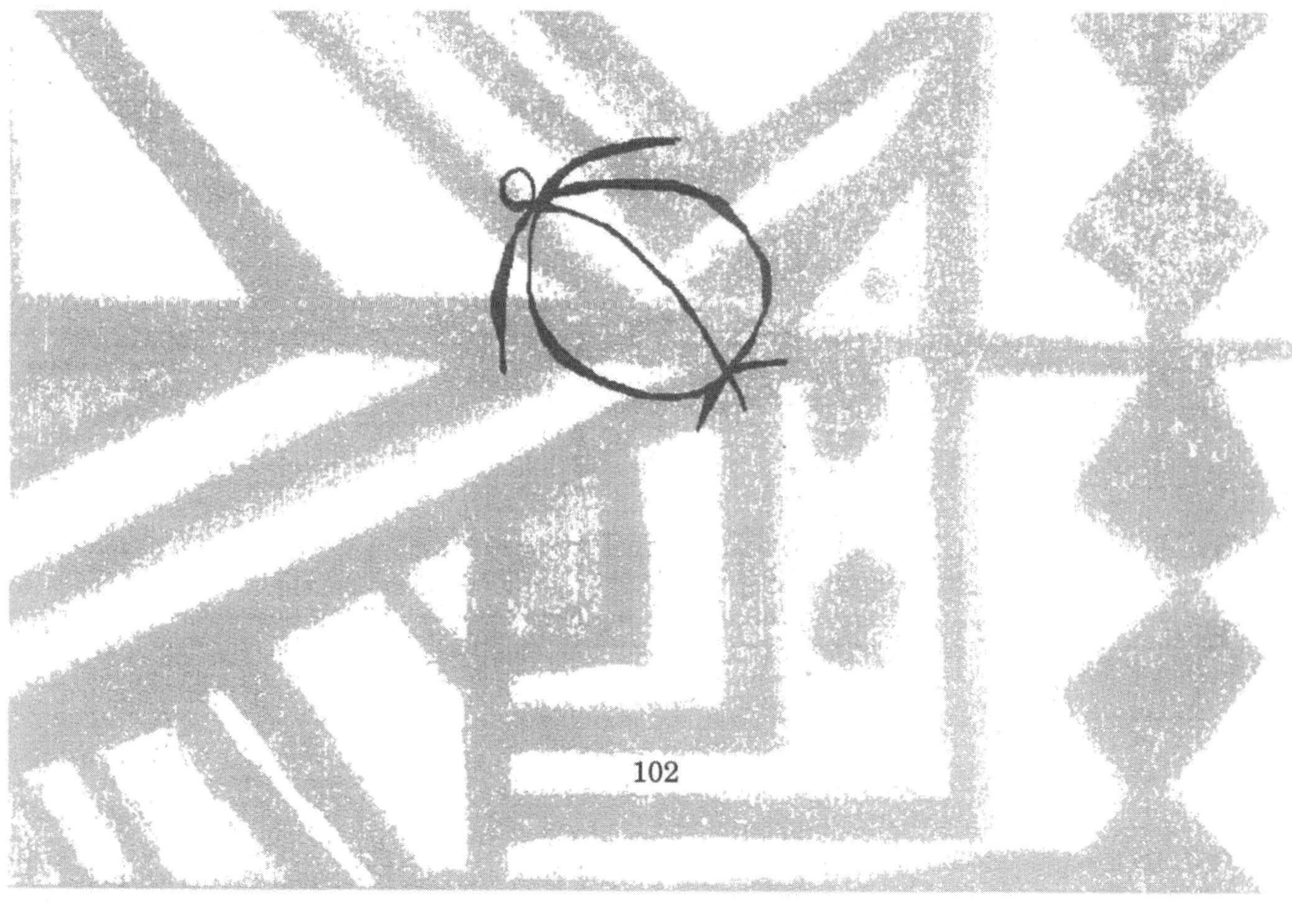

Ua Like Nō A Like

F Wahine

Alice Everett

BX
1/2 BV
Pau

Ua Like Nō A Like

"My Heart`s Choice" is composer Alice Everett's interpretation of the title for this early 1900's song. It has lyrical expressions like "sweet constancy," and like most Hawaiian love songs, alludes to nature. My great grandmother, Helen Desha Beamer, made the first recording of this song in the mid 1900's, for Columbia Records. It has had a recent (1997) release as a choral piece by students of the Kamehameha Schools in Honolulu, Hawai'i.

Performance Notes

Play this immortal love song with a soft, gentle cadence such as you would use to whisper in the ear of your beloved.

Pickup and Measures 1–2 As you can see, this introduction uses double stops on the first and third strings; in fact, you'll encounter almost all of the common double stops in ***F Wahine Tuning*** playing just this short passage! The final chord (beat one, measure 3), an F major, is home in this tuning.

Play these measures without a strong rhythm, and use quick rolling arpeggios to sound each chord.

Measure 3 The first chord is a C7; use your index finger on the first string, ring finger on the second, and middle finger on the third string. Immediately shift your hand position, placing your index finger at the 10th fret, second string, and your ring finger at the 12th fret on the third string. This position lets you slide down to the double stop at beat three, then back up to the 12th fret on beat four, moving your index finger to the first string.

Measure 4 Place your fingers for this F major chord as follows: index at the 8th fret, first string; middle at the 9th fret, second string; and ring finger, 10th fret, third string. This is a basic fingering throughout this arrangement, so take a moment to commit it to memory. Now use your pinky to play the pull-off.

Measure 6 Although it isn't notated, the easiest way to play the figure on beat one is by using the same fingering as for the F major chord in measure 4. Once again, use your pinky for the pull-off.

Measures 7–8 Simply a variation of the melody from measures 3 and 4.

Measure 11 You begin an ascending series of double stops with a C7, resolving back to the tonic on beat three of the next measure. Try to separate each note ever so slightly by letting your thumb and fingers roll off the strings.

Measure 15 Barre across all six strings for this Bb chord, releasing it just before beat three.

Measure 16 Set up a partial barre across the top four strings and pull off from your ring finger to the barre.

Measures 16–17 This is almost the same passage as the introduction; notice that you reach the last double stop just slightly ahead of the final downbeat.

G Sixth Tuning
D G D G B E

This unusual tuning combines some of the best features of *Taro Patch* and standard tuning. Essentially a G major chord with the addition of the sixth tone (the open E string), ***G Sixth Tuning*** is readily accessible to guitarists used to playing in standard tuning. Like *C Wahine*, the upper strings retain their normal pitch relationships, so scales and chord voices have a familiar feel.

To tune to *G Sixth Tuning* from standard, lower your fifth string a whole step to G (an octave below your third string) and slack the bass down to D, an octave below the fourth string. To check your tuning, press the first string at the third fret and strum across all the strings to sound a G major chord.

From *Taro Patch*, simply raise the first string from D up to E.

And from *C Wahine*, raise the sixth string from C to D.

Studying how these tunings relate to each other will greatly enhance your enjoyment of slack key guitar.

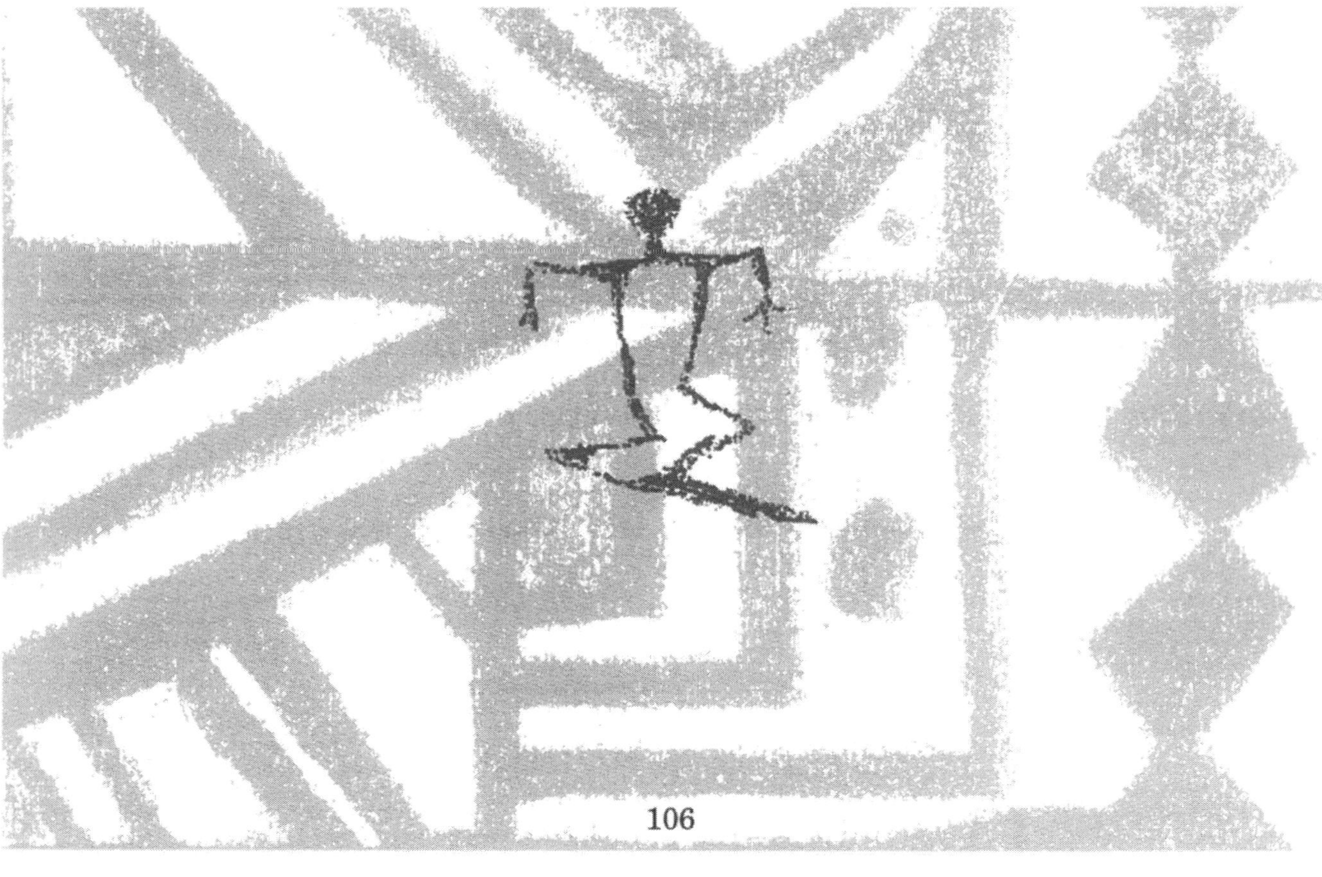

Hi'ilawe

G Sixth Tuning *cresc.* Mrs. Kuakini

14
17
20
ritard
23
Pau

Hi'ilawe

Hi'ilawe is a beautiful cascading waterfall located in the valley of Waipi'o on the Island of Hawai'i. Here in Hawai'i, there is a unique rhythm to life. Even the waterfalls have a pulse as they fall from great heights to sea level.

There are many species of birds in Waipi'o and one must be careful of how one behaves, lest they observe something unusual. ***Hi'ilawe*** *is an old song that tells the story of a young woman who has a love affair in the spray of the waterfall. The song reminds us that birds love to chatter and with their incessant gossiping, rumors are spread throughout the entire valley.*

Performance notes

The song, built around the five or ten bar structure so common in Hawaiian music, is a slack key standard.

Measures 1–2 Keola uses a beautiful variation of the classic ***Hi'ilawe*** turnaround. Play the slur as a rapid hammer/pull triplet with a flick of your ring finger.

Measures 3–4 To play a crescendo (noted ***cresc.***) start off softly, then build in volume and intensity until you reach the end of the phrase. A phrase is a musical sentence or statement; bars 3 and 4 comprise one complete phrase. Using a crescendo makes this part of the song more dramatic.

Measure 5 Note the double stop slur or hammer-on. Up to this point we've only seen hammer-ons involving a single string; here you hammer both strings simultaneously. Try not to rush the tempo of the slurred passage. Use the 3rd and 4th fingers of the left hand for the hammer-on, and listen carefully to the sound that you are making. You'll want to hear both notes clearly.

Measures 11–19 Keola is known for his inventive bridges, short musical sections that connect the main parts of an arrangement. This extended passage almost stands as a composition in its own right. Use it as a springboard for developing your own musical statement.

Starting at bar 16 there are more slurs (in this case, hammer-ons). Isolate these left hand finger movements; take them out of the context of the piece and play them slowly and smoothly. After they start feeling comfortable, build up to tempo and insert them into the body of the piece. This is always an excellent approach to problematic passages.

Another characteristic of Keola's style is his use of his thumb to play melody notes. Try to practice each measure by itself, gradually adding more pieces until you can execute the entire bridge.

Measure 20 The melody begins again. Play it one time, and then *ritard* through the turnarounds to the final chord.

Double Slack Tuning

D G D F♯ B D

Also known as *G Wahine, **Double Slack***, is a popular and versatile tuning that lends itself particularly well to slurs and harmonics. Like all *Wahine* tunings, it doesn't sound complete until you press down on one or more strings. This is because of the major seventh interval, in this case an F♯.

Hawaiian Slack Key guitarists make masterful use of this interval by hammering on back to the tonic. Listen to how masters Sonny Chillingworth, Raymond Kāne, and Ledward Ka'apana play in *Double Slack* and you'll get chicken skin for sure!

The easiest way to get to *Double Slack* is from *Taro Patch*; simply lower your third string one half step from a G down to an F♯. Check your tuning by fretting the third string at the first fret and strumming a G major chord.

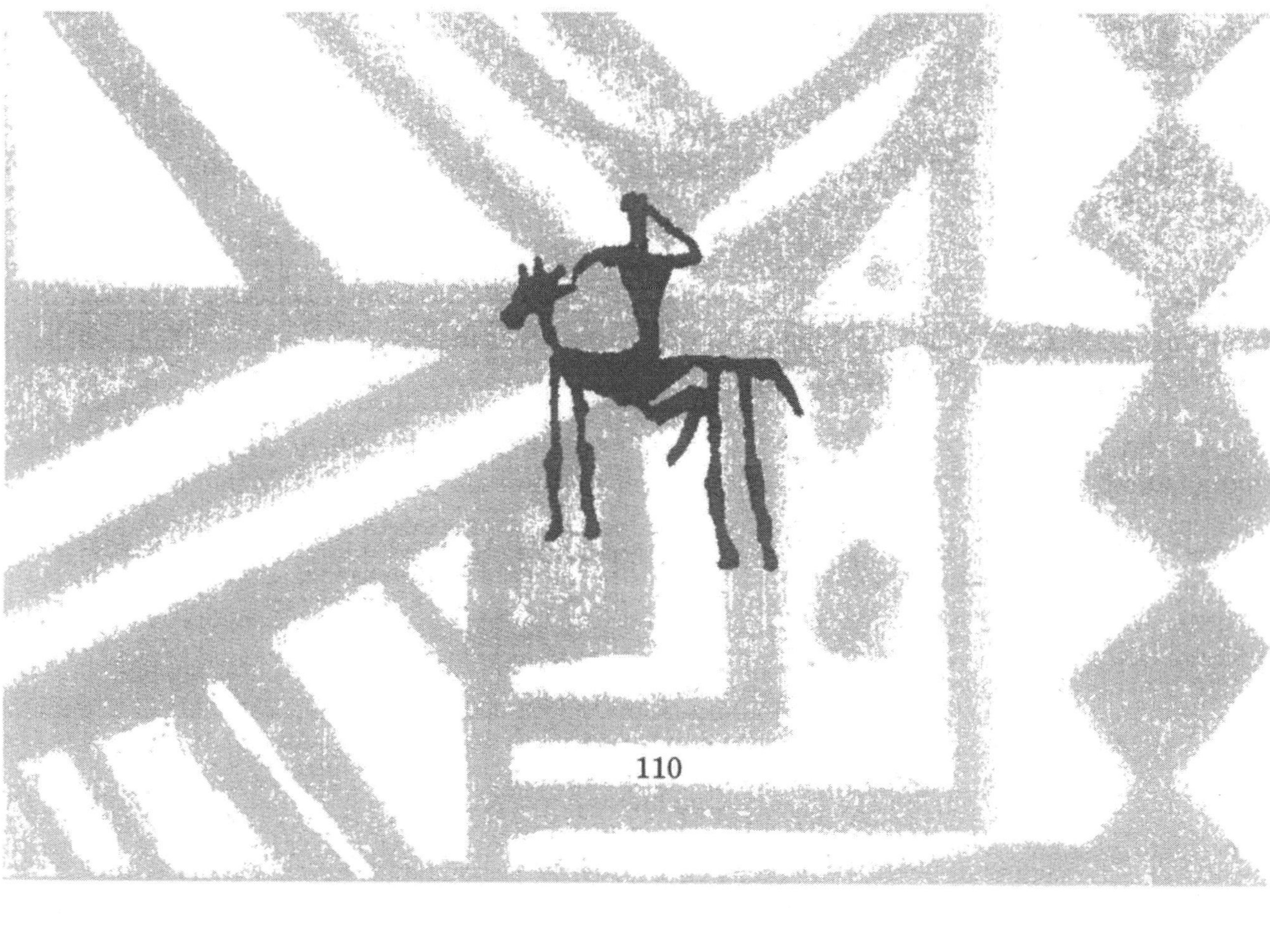

Playful Pōpoki

Double Slack

Mark Nelson

Pau

Playful Pōpoki

Pōpoki *is Hawaiian for cat—the name originated when Islanders overheard a missionary wife comforting her bedraggled pet after a particularly bad landing: "Poor, poor kitty."*

This original tune of Mark's was inspired by the antics of Slippers, Moana and Keola's cat. Picture a happy kitty with a piece of string as you wind through the quick slurs, loping rhythm, and twisty melody.

Performance Notes

Measures 1 and 3 Keep one eye on the notation to see which notes are played with the thumb. The thumb keeps a steady quarter note pulse throughout the song; cross over with your index finger to pluck the fourth string for the hammer-on following beat two.

Measure 2 The key to this song is to create a smooth series of hammer-ons and pull-offs. Pull off from G to F♯ on beat two and follow through with a hammer back to the G on beat three; you should be able to hear each eighth note distinctly. Make sure the final hammer-on coincides with the plucked note on beat three.

Measures 6–7 Even though it isn't notated, life will be easier if you keep your index finger on the second string, first fret for most of the next two measures.

Measure 8 Think of the eighth notes as a continuation of the previous measure.

Measures 9–10 Try to achieve a smooth flow between the numerous pull-offs and hammer-ons; all of the eighth notes flow smoothly into one another across the bar lines.

Measures 11–12 Just a variation of measure one, with a quick hammer-on to the first melody note.

Measure 13 The thumb breaks from its steady pattern to play some melody notes. Notice how this brings some syncopation into the arrangement.

Measures 14–20 More variations on the theme. Again, strive for a smooth, even flow of notes whether they are plucked or slurred.

Measure 25 After you hammer down to the first fret, second string with your index finger, play the triplets as a very rapid series of plucked note, hammer-on, pull-off with your middle finger. Use your pinky to reach up to the fourth fret and pull off back to the open string.

Measure 26 Start with harmonics at the seventh fret—any finger will do; then execute another rapid pluck-hammer-pull series with your middle finger.

Playful Pōpoki is fairly typical of the way slack key guitarists shape a tune in *Double Slack* tuning. Almost every great player has a show piece tune in this popular tuning; listen to Sonny Chillingworth's *Whee Haw Swing* and Raymond Kāne's *Punehele* for two wonderful examples.

This arrangement is purposefully brief; after you have mastered these variations, create some of your own. A good place to start would be to play measures one through four, then find your own variations for the next six measures. Remember to come back to the tonic in measures eight and ten.

Ka Makani ʻOluʻolu
The Pleasant Wind

Double Slack

Keola Beamer

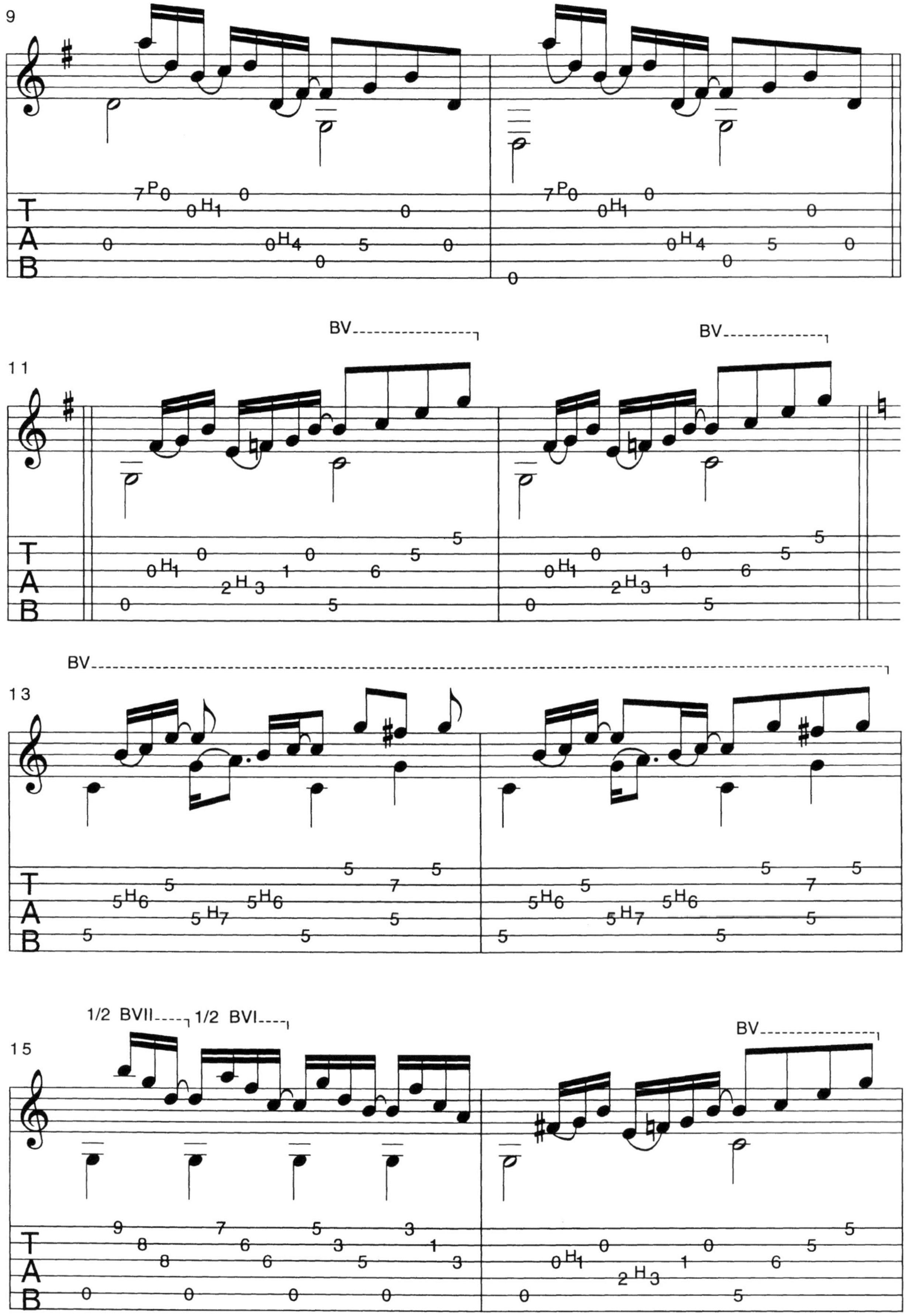
9
11
BV
BV
13
BV
15
1/2 BVII
1/2 BVI
BV

BV
BVII
17
BVII
19
21
23

ritard

Ka Makani ʻOluʻolu

Ka makani *is Hawaiian for the wind. In the old days in Hawaiʻi, the wind was not just the wind. When Laʻamaomao (the keeper of winds) brings wind to the district of Kohala, on the Big Island, it is called the* ʻApaʻapaʻa, *a gusty breeze, coming in spurts, raising spirals of dust. There are also names for the general qualities of the wind in Hawaiʻi.* Moani Ke ʻAla *is a soft, fragrance bearing wind. The* Malanai *is a gentle, wafting breeze.*

I wrote this song for the wind that blew through the back yard of my home in Alewa Heights when I was a young man. ʻOluʻolu *means pleasing, refreshing, or kind.*

Performance Notes

Hang on to your hat, because this wind is going to give you a wild ride. Keola's original tune is full of twists and turns, so take a deep breath and let's get started.

Essentially based on the same form as *Aunty Alice Nāmakelua Slack Key, Matt's Bounce*, and *Playful Pōpoki*, ***Ka Makani ʻOluʻolu*** is a challenging slack key tour de force.

Measures 1–5 This is the basic form of the tune. Keep a half note bass against the myriad slurs and harmonics and you will be OK. Best not to take it too fast; things get scary pretty quick.

Measure 3 Use your index and middle fingers for the slurs on the first two strings (frets 6 and 7); then move to your ring finger for the 8th fret, third string.

Measure 4 Take advantage of the open fourth string to shift up the neck. Ready? There are several ways to play the quick series of slurs; one is to start with your index finger at fret 11. Use your middle finger for the next note (fret 12, first string) and immediately shift to the second string with the same finger. That puts your ring finger in position for the note at fret 13; a slight shift and your index finger reaches the 10th fret.

With your middle finger, reach up to the third string, fret 11; and maintain the relative position as you slide up the finger board. Then do it all over again in the next measure. Five measures down, twenty-eight to go.

Measures 6–10 A variation of the original theme. Nothing too challenging. In measures 8 and 9, you reverse the usual bass pattern, playing the higher note on beat one.

Measures 11–12 A two bar bridge; the hammer up to the F natural (fourth string, fret 3) sets up a modulation to the key of C.

Measures 13–14 Now you are in the key of C major. Just to make things interesting, your bass changes to a quarter note pattern. Play the lick while holding a barre at fret 5.

Measure 15 Keola sets up a beautiful descending pattern; use partial barres and try to connect each note. Remember the Hawaiian principle of *nahenahe*.

Measures 18–19 Another two bar bridge, this time to set up the modulation back to G. Look closely, the rhythm of the basic figure changes slightly on the G chords.

Measures 20–24 Simply a variation of the original pattern. You can relax for now.

Measures 25–28 Nothing like a little four bar funk vamp to liven up a tune. It's not as hard as it looks, so don't panic. The notation is only one suggestion of how to finger this passage, so feel free to try your own. Keola and Mark don't do it the same way, either.

Mark favors using his thumb for the bass runs in measures 25 & 27. Notice that they are just the same lick played on different strings.

Measures 26 & 28 can be played using a quarter note bass pulse; they look more complicated than they are.

Measures 29–33 Congratulations, you are back in familiar territory! This is just like the beginning of the song. At measure 33, slow down to bring everything to a beautiful conclusion.

Ka Makani ʻOluʻolu brings together many of the different facets of *kī hōʻalu*. In form, it relates to the beginnings of slack key: a repeating pattern that moves from the tonic chord to the dominant chord and back, with an extra turnaround thrown in for good measure. We have had the chance to play a number of arrangements that share this form; keep your ear open and you will hear many more.

The song is a highly personal statement, evocative of the love of the land and nature so dear to the Hawaiian heart. Picture a cooling breeze as it spirals through the foliage towards where you sit, thankful for a respite from the tropical sun. Can you hear the leaves murmur as it moves closer?

It is also very much a show piece for the slack key guitar, carefully crafted to fully exploit the possibilities of ***Double Slack*** tuning. Keola uses every trick in the book: slurs, bass runs, modulations, theme and variations, chimes. Truly a masterwork. But the hot licks never get in the way of the story.

And it is full of youthful energy and exuberance. As you play, think about how your life informs every note you make.

Ka Hā O Ka Mokuna

Section Four

Although much of the emphasis in the past few years has been on solo playing, slack key is very much part of a family or group playing tradition. In the old days, Hawaiians living in isolated rural areas made their own music by the warm light of a kerosene lantern. Even today, just about any party or family outing will be accompanied by the gentle sound of one or more guitars and *'ukulele.* The hills still ring with real, homemade music.

For this final chapter, Keola and Mark present a selection of duet arrangements. There is no better way to play music than with a friend, so tune up those guitars and go to it. Don't worry if you don't have anyone to play with, drop in the CD and jam along!

These last songs bring together everything we've looked at so far. Have fun!

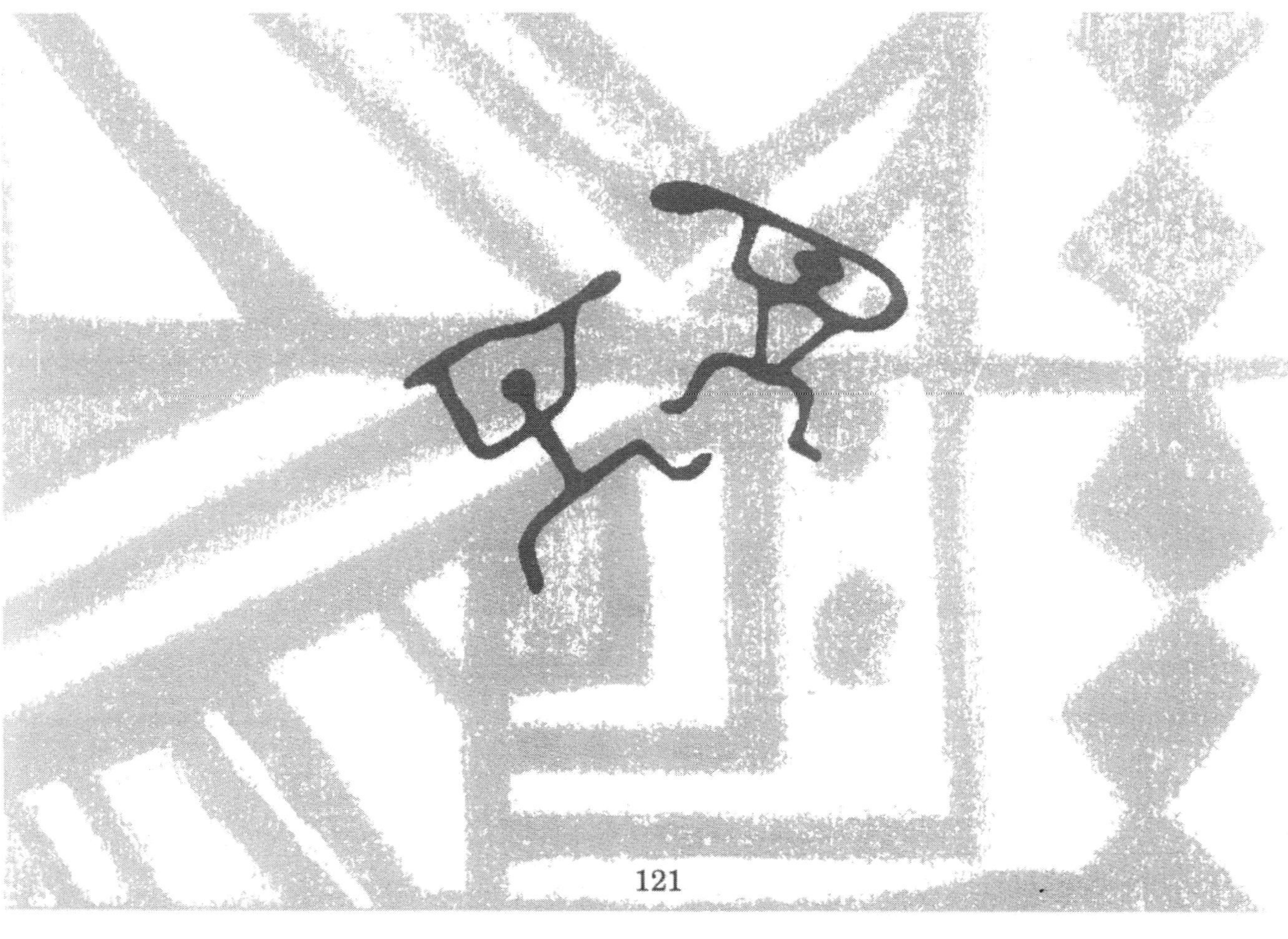

Then everybody looks at you funny

How would you go about playing these songs with two or three people? Would you find tunings that were related, or would someone play it in standard tuning and someone else in slack key?

Well, you'd probably not want to do something in a tuning that's too off the wall; you'd do "C" or "G" or something. Then So and So would bring up their 'ukulele. *Generally they would know the song, and you are going to play the same chords. As a common thing, you'd sing a verse, then you'd lean over to Uncle So and So and you'd say, "Ah, take one." Then he plays a little solo thing, then you get back and sing the second verse and he goes, "Take one!" and you take one, you know....*

I think jazz is sort of like that, a little bit. You get this little space in the limelight for you to blow a little bit, then you all go back to the root of the song.

And you're improvising....

Within the chord structure.

And occasionally a little *without* the chord structure....

Yeah! Then everybody looks at you funny!

Akāka Falls
Duet

C Wahine

Helen Parker

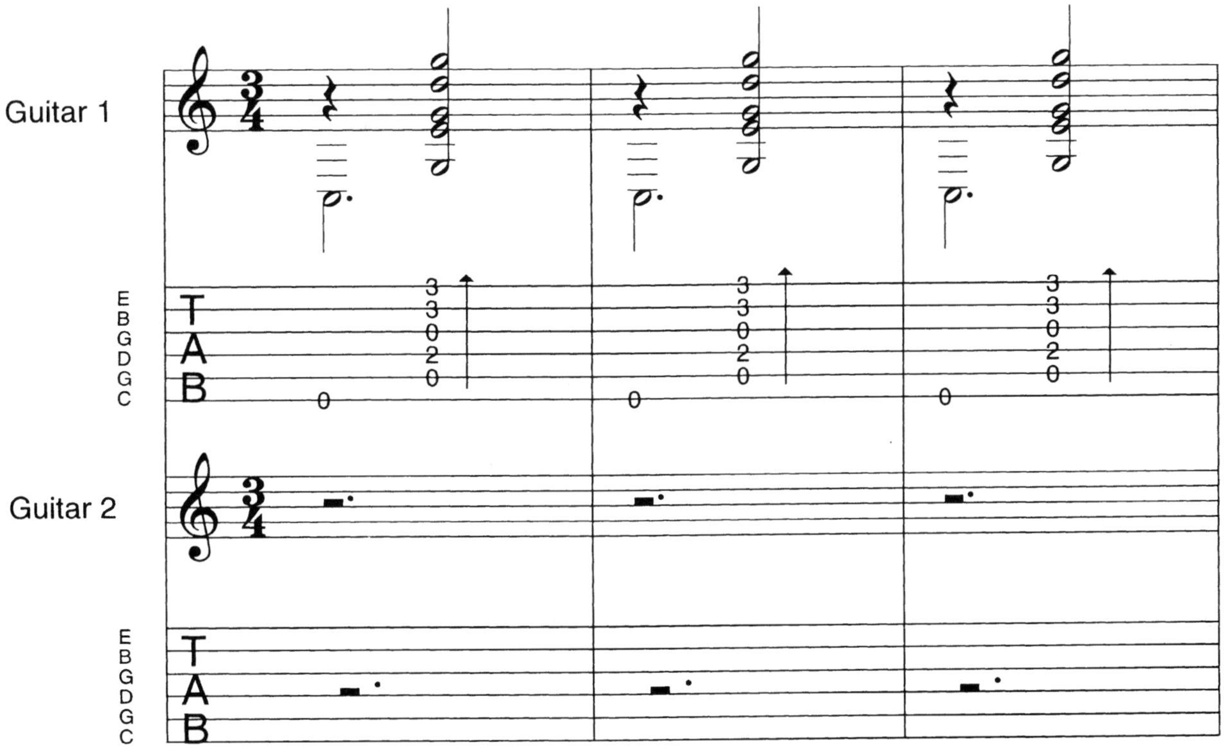

8
12
BV
BV
BVIII

16
BV

20
BI
BIII
1.

24
2.
Pau
Pau

Akāka Falls

Akāka Falls is a real place outside the little town of Hilo, along the Hāmākua coast on the Island of Hawai'i. I used to visit this area with my grandfather and we'd eat our bento box lunches, watching the water cascade down the rocky precipice. Beneath us, beautiful, dark currents of water seemed to move mysteriously through the verdant foliage. I still remember the sound of the first drops of summer rain, splattering on the broad green leaves.

Keola's Performance Notes

This is an easy piece in ***C Wahine*** that contains some surprisingly wonderful elements. Start off by listening to the CD of the complete duet with me playing the first guitar part and Mark playing the second. Take a look at how the parts work together by studying the duet notation. A good way to approach this guitar piece would be to learn the second guitar part first. It is the least difficult of the two parts. Play it smoothly from the TAB a couple of times, trying for an even tempo and clarity of tone. Then put on the CD and play along. Set up the tracking so I play the first guitar part and you play the second in real time.

Pretty nice huh?

Now take a look at the first guitar part. In the first four measures, there is a beautiful chord that I call "the water chord." It's an evocative expression of the mysterious water currents that we have here in Hawai'i. Play these chords gently with the thumb on the open 6th string and the index finger of the right hand strumming down, in one stroke—through the first string. Try to do this smoothly, slowly separating the individual notes a bit. Clearly, the melody notes are played on the first 3 strings, the beautiful low bass C's and G's create a reflective pool from which the melody surfaces.

This is the heart of the Hawaiian slack key guitar. The beautiful overtones and coloration of sound create a radiant space in the air around you. Learn to be in that space, using the palette of these colors and tunings to begin to tell your story.

The more one seeks to exist in this "space," the more comfortable it becomes to be there. It is a wonderful irony of the guitar that the more we understand it, the less it exists. It's as if the mastery of the instrument leads to its own dissolution. The better you get at controlling the guitar, the more invisible it becomes. When the instrument finally does not exist any more, when it is totally beneath your consciousness, then all that is left is you. You'll begin to hear the story of your own life, within the context of that beautiful, radiant space. Often this achievement surprises us. It is far beyond words. It is, finally, music.

Kī Hō'alu Mischief

Guitar 1: F Wahine

Guitar 2: Taro Patch, slacked to F

Keola Beamer and Mark Nelson

1.

2.

25
TAB
29
TAB

33
37

48
T
A
B
T
A
B
52
T
A
B
T
A
B

62
66
TAB

ritard
78
81
Pau
Pau

Kī Hōʻalu Mischief

One evening after dinner Mark and I were sitting around trading guitar licks in the studio, when for some reason, we decided to take a little musical trip to the Caribbean. Perhaps the food we had eaten was just a bit too spicy. In preparation for our journey we added a few classic slack key riffs and set sail with me in F Wahine and Mark in Taro Patch slacked down to F.

Sometimes with the guitar, you just have to have a little fun.

Performance Notes

The title says it all—two guitarists captured in the act of goofing off. Although our parts were originally improvised, we tried to standardize them for the recording so you could get in on the fun. The structure of the piece is pretty simple; Keola plays a lovely introduction, we vamp for four bars, and then all bets are off.

Keola takes the first solo; there's a short bridge; then Mark takes the second solo. We briefly return to the top of the tune, and finally play a typical slack key turnaround. What could be simpler?

Guitar #1

Let's look at Keola's part first. It starts out easy enough, but quickly evolves into a blazing showpiece of syncopation and slurs. Even though we present a somewhat simplified version of his performance in the TAB, be forewarned: prepare yourself for some seriously fun guitar playing.

Measures 1–5 Play this sweet little introduction with a great deal of feeling. Let each tone ring as long as you can.

Measures 5– 8 Keola came up with this cool trick of hammering on to a note without picking it; in effect using some of his left hand fingers to tap and pull off, while the other fingers maintain their normal roles. For the vamp, sound the bass note with your thumb. Then pluck the note at fret 10 on the third string. Nothing unusual here. Next, pluck the open second string and immediately hammer down to the third string, 9th fret. Use enough force to clearly sound the note.

On beat four, play the double stop with your thumb and index finger, and hammer back to fret 10.

Take plenty time to work this whole sequence through; it defines the tone of this piece. Not only are you tapping with your left hand, but you need to learn to keep an unusual rhythm with your thumb.

As you encounter each new challenge, stop and practice just one or two measures until they flow smoothly; gradually integrating them into the parts you have already mastered.

Measure 10 There are a couple of interesting things going on here. In the first place, the bass changes from playing on beats one and four to a highly syncopated pattern. Notice that the final note is sounded by pulling off on the third string. You'll encounter this technique in several other places.

Measures 13–16 Check out the inventive way Keola found to play an otherwise simple turnaround. Use your pinky for the hammer-on to the fifth fret.

Measure 19 Keola at his most playful. Pay attention to which notes are picked with your fingers, which are sounded as pull-offs, and which are plucked with your thumb.

Measure 22 Keola "ghosts" a hammer-on from the open first string in this and most of the following measures. It's pretty hard to hear on the recording, listen for a subtle shift in the timing. Like all similar figures, we've notated it as a single note preceded by an "H". You can ignore the hammer until you are thoroughly familiar with the piece.

Other than that, it's smooth sailing until measure 50.

Measure 50 Keola repeats what he played earlier (measures 17 through 49) as his accompaniment to Mark's solo.

Measures 76–81 A repeat of the opening vamp. Gradually slow the tempo.

Measures 82–83 This is a 2/5/1 turnaround, so called because the chords, built from the second and fifth scale degree of the key, turn the music back to the tonic. In this case, the chords are a G9 and Csus7, leading to an F major.

Notice that Keola's final harmonic doesn't resolve unless both guitars are playing.

Guitar #2

Mark's guitar takes on several different roles; moving from a supporting rhythmic vamp played on harmonics, to a syncopated bass line, to a lead melody, and back. By now you should be familiar with most of the techniques, so we'll just look at a couple of things.

Measures 17–21 The bass line features a rhythm from the Caribbean known as the *Calypso Clave*. This syncopated rhythm is found throughout the part, so make sure you get it down pat.

Measures 22– 28 Same feel, different strings.

Measures 30–31 Here's the *clave* again, now played by the fingers against a steady four beat bass.

From here on it's pretty much straight ahead. You'll notice some familiar licks, like the *Taro Patch* turnarounds that keep cropping up. Watch for some of the more wicked syncopation; remember to take your time and isolate any difficult passages.

As you can see, the structure of the tune is quite simple. Essentially, it's strung together from short sections, with an extra turnaround every now and then. Once you have a handle on it, try improvising your own parts to play along with the recordings.

And be sure to try out some different tunings. For example, you could take *Double Slack* down to F; or tune to one of the C tunings and capo at the fourth fret.

Kī Hōʻalu Mischief is what happens when two good friends get together to talk story with their guitars. Come join us.

Tiare Tahiti

Guitar #1 F Wahine, capo 2
Guitar #2 Taro Patch

Traditional Tahitian

10
H P P H
H
BV
14

BIV
BII
19
23
BV
BV

27
H P
31
BV

BIV
BII
36
Repeat for solos and fade out
BV
41

Tiare Tahiti

The tiare *is the Tahitian gardenia, a beautiful white flower that is delicately scented. If you have ever been to French Polynesia, you will most likely understand the attachment that native people have for this blossom. Deep within the islands where the moonlight casts shadows, the scent of the* tiare *permeates the night air. In a most unexplainable way, it becomes a part of your own existence.*

When you are away from those beautiful islands, you might recall the fragrance of that flower; and when you do, you will feel a longing in your heart, a deep desire, to return again to that place where the wind whispers and the tiare *breathes in the night air.*

Performance Notes

One day Keola mentioned he knew a lovely song that might make a good duet for the book. He taught Mark the melody and they sat down in the recording studio to see where it would lead them. This beautiful spontaneous arrangement was created right from the heart.

Tiare Tahiti sums up everything we can teach you about the Hawaiian slack key guitar. Rather than give you a detailed, measure by measure breakdown of what each guitarist did, we ask you to listen carefully to the recording. Hear how each guitarist interprets the melody, pay attention to how the two guitars work together. When you pick up your guitar and play, be aware of the feeling that comes through the vibrating strings into the room.

Keola's guitar is tuned to ***F Wahine***, he uses a capo to bring it into the key of G major. The TAB is written relative to the capo'd position; hence the number 2 indicates a note two frets higher than the capo, not the second fret of the guitar.

Both Keola and Mark make extensive use of their thumbs to set up syncopated bass lines, pay careful attention to the direction of the note stems for guidance. For the sake of clarity, many of the ornaments, slides and arpeggios have been left out of the TAB. By now, you have acquired the knowledge to ornament the melody in your own unique way.

Take your time to learn the subtleties and nuances of this arrangement, and then play along with one of the recorded parts. Use your feelings to guide your fingers and let your aloha flow. From here, it becomes your story.

What It All Means

This music has soul. It's important to understand how much meaning you can get from doing this.

This is not flipping a coin or something. This is not a game of chance. This is, a little bit, the story of life. When you press on those strings and learn a little bit about what's going on, the story of you comes forth. It's your life.... the things that happen to you.

The guitar is the campfire, and you are the story.

Musicians often joke about "You play music because you have to." You have no choice. That seems to be the difference between a musician and someone who plays nose flute or guitar or whatever, but doesn't really have it.

Hey, don't diss the nose flute, man!

Sorry.

You get bitten by this thing, It's like a virus. And pretty soon.... Look what has happened to you: you felt the music in your heart, and it sort of powered you, empowered you, to learn more about this thing. Now you're hanging in Hawai'i with one of the players. Pretty soon, as the days go by, you're gonna slack down a little bit.... your lifestyle, literally. Your heartbeat will kinda just.... you stay with the waves; you know, walking on the beach for a few days, and you'll get that rhythm thing happening, and....

It's easy. That's the word nahenahe, *that soft soothing that it does to your heart when you listen to it. You could be a really uptight human being and get into this music and it could save you! It has that wonderful ability to make peace in your heart.*

"For only $19.95!"

I'm gonna hit you with my damned nose flute!

I see it in people who migrate to Hawai'i from the west coast. I've worked with guys, and they come out sort of very "OK, Let's get this done. Yadda yadda yadda," you know, very uptight. And after a few days, the posture kind of slouches a little bit, and the pants get wrinkled.... and pretty soon, you know, it's "Yeah, we'll get to it."

Life just sort of takes on a different rhythm, and the further you go into Polynesia, the more exotic that transformation becomes.

Tahiti.... the world's most beautiful people.... and women, and water.... and it's quite common for people to give up their homes, their mortgages, their lives and the western world and they just disappear in this beautiful relaxed new life. All the rest of that stuff just starts melting.

So, we're telling people to melt into their guitars.

(Laughs). Yeah, we want them to understand that it ain't just pounding on the strings. Good stuff happens.

Annotated Discography

Many of the songs Keola and Mark teach in this book have been recorded by the great Hawaiian masters of the slack key guitar. The following annotated discography, compiled by George "Keoki" Winston, musician and founder of Dancing Cat Records, is included to help you get more enjoyment out of your study of this wonderful guitar tradition.

The best way to learn to play slack key is to listen; as you become familiar with the many different interpretations of these classic songs, you will see how the contribution of each individual is so important to the music.

Akāka Falls

Keola Beamer (under title *Ka Wailele O Akāka*) from the recording MAUNA KEA–WHITE MOUNTAIN JOURNAL (Dancing Cat 38011) in ***C Wahine Tuning*** (C-G-D-G-B-E), playing in keys of F and C. *Wahine* is a tuning that contains a major 7th note.

Leonard Kwan from the recording THE OLD WAY (Tradewinds Records 1128) in ***F Wahine Tuning*** (C-F-C-G-C-E).

Ledward Ka'apana & Bob Brozman from the recording KĪKĀ KĪLĀ MEETS KĪ HŌ'ALU (Dancing Cat 38031) with Led playing slack key guitar in standard tuning (E-A-D-G-B-E), and Bob playing acoustic steel guitar in ***Taro Patch***. Both are playing in the key of F

'Alekoki

Cyril Pahinui & Bob Brozman for an upcoming recording on Dancing Cat Records with Cyril playing slack key guitar in a ***D Major Tuning*** (D-A-D-F♯-A-D), and Bob on acoustic steel guitar in ***Taro Patch*** (D-G-D-G-B-D), playing in the key of D.

Aunty Alice Nāmakelua Slack Key

Keola Beamer, recorded as *Nāmakelua's Slack Key* for a future Dancing Cat release, in ***B♭ Wahine Tuning.*** Also included on Keola's Homespun video, THE ART OF HAWAIIAN SLACK KEY GUITAR, as *A Grandmother's Wish* in ***B♭ Wahine***. ***B♭ Wahine*** tunings are basically C tunings with the whole guitar tuned down two half-steps with the two lowest-pitched strings reversed in their roles. In the C tuning, the tonic is on the lowest-pitched 6th string, and the 5th note of the scale is on the 5th string. In B♭ tuning, the tonic is now on the 5th string, and the 5th note of the scale is on the 6th string. Therefore, a B♭ tuning is a C tuning with the four highest-pitched strings tuned down, and the two lowest-pitched strings tuned up.

Hame Pila

Gabby Pahinui from the recording GABBY ("The Brown Album," Panini Records 1002) in a ***C Wahine Tuning*** (C-G-E-G-B-E) tuned down to sound in key of A.

Hi'ilawe

The two earliest versions of Philip "Gabby" Pahinui (1921-1980) recording this song have been reissued on the CD, THE HISTORY OF SLACK KEY GUITAR (Hana Ola Records 24000). Gabby always played this in a ***C Wahine Tuning*** (C-G-E-G-B-E) called ***Hi'ilawe*** or ***Gabby's Hi'ilawe Tuning*** because it was recorded first and most prominently by Gabby Pahinui. Gabby has been called the father of the modern slack key era because he made the first slack key recordings, starting in 1946, and he has been the most influential slack key guitarist ever.

Gabby Pahinui from the recording PURE GABBY (Hula Records 567) in ***C Wahine Tuning*** (C-G-E-G-B-E).

Gabby Pahinui from the recording GABBY ("The Brown Album," Panini Records 1002) ***in C Wahine*** (C-G-E-G-B-E).

Keola Beamer from the recording MAUNA KEA–WHITE MOUNTAIN JOURNAL (Dancing Cat 38011) in ***G Sixth Tuning*** (D-G-D-G-B-E).

Sonny Chillingworth from the recording SONNY SOLO (Dancing Cat 38005) in ***Modified C Wahine Tuning*** (C-G-D-G-B-D).

Ray Kāne from the recording WA'AHILA (Dancing Cat 38002) in a ***C Wahine Tuning*** (C-G-D-G-B-E) slacked down to B♭.

Ray Kāne from the recording NANAKULI'S RAYMOND KĀNE (Tradewinds Records 1130) in ***G Wahine Tuning*** (***Double Slack***) (D-G-D-F♯-B-D).

Cyril Pahinui from the recording NIGHT MOON (Dancing Cat 38030) in the ***C Major Tuning*** (C-G-E-G-C-E).

George Kuo (under the title *Old Hi'ilawe*) from the recording NAHENAHE (Hula Records 576) in ***C Wahine Tuning*** (C-G-E-G-B-E).

Led Ka'apana from the recording LED LIVE (Dancing Cat 38008) in standard tuning (E-A-D-G-B-E), playing in key of C.

Haunani Kahalewai from the recording HAUNANI–THE VOICE OF HAWAI'I (Decca Records 74561—out of print). Another version is on 49th State Records #181-B (78 rpm) and the same track is on 49th State Records EP-4 (out of print— to be reissued). Both versions are in a ***D Wahine Tuning*** (D-A-D-F♯-A-C♯).

James "Bla" Pahinui on an upcoming recording on Dancing Cat Records in ***Dropped D Tuning*** (D-A-D-G-B-E).

Hilo March

Cyril Pahinui & Bob Brozman (in a medley with *Kēlā Mea Whiffa*) from the recording FOUR HANDS, SWEET AND HOT (Dancing Cat 38048) with Cyril playing slack key guitar in ***D Major Tuning*** (D-A-D-F♯-A-D), and Bob on acoustic steel guitar in ***Taro Patch*** tuned up to the key of A and playing in the key of D (bar on 5th fret is the tonic).

Kahumoku Brothers from the recording SWEET AND SASSY–HAWAIIAN SLACK KEY STYLING, VOL. 1 (Kahumoku Brothers 1005—out of print) in ***Taro Patch***, tuned down to key of F.

Hula O Makee

Cyril Pahinui & Bob Brozman from the recording FOUR HANDS, SWEEET AND HOT (Dancing Cat 38048) with Cyril playing slack key guitar in the ***C Major Tuning*** (C-G-E-G-C-E) tuned down 2 half steps to the key of Bb, and Bob playing acoustic steel guitar in ***Taro Patch*** (D-G-D-G-B-D) tuned up 3 half steps to sound in the key of Bb.

Ray Kāne from the recording PUNAHELE (Dancing Cat 38001) in ***Taro Patch***, tuned down to F♯.

Cyril Pahinui from the recording KA HO'OILINA MAU...THE LEGACY CONTINUES (Poki Records 9062) in the ***C Major Tuning***, in the key of C.

Isalei

Gabby Pahinui (as part of song called *Farewell Medley*) from the recording PURE GABBY (Hula Records 567) in an ***F Wahine Tuning*** (F-C-E-G-C-E), known as ***Gabby's F*** because it was recorded first and most prominently by the late great slack key guitarist Philip "Gabby" Pahinui.

James "Bla" Pahinui from the recording MANA (Dancing Cat 38033) in ***Dropped D Tuning*** (D-A-D-G-B-D).

Kāhuli Aku

Keola & Kapono Beamer (as part of a medley with *Pūpū Hinuhinu* and *Ka Huelo 'Opae*) from the recording THIS IS OUR ISLAND HOME–WE ARE HER SONS (Music of Polynesia Records 29000) with Keola in ***C Wahine Tuning*** (C-G-D-G-B-E), and Kapono in ***Taro Patch***, playing in the key of C.

Keola Beamer (as part of a medley with *Green Rose Hula* and *Kananaka*) for an upcoming recording on Dancing Cat Records in ***F Wahine Tuning*** (C-F-C-G-C-E), often called *Leonard's F* because it was recorded first and most prominently by the great slack key guitarist Leonard Kwan.

Kī Hōʻalu

Leonard Kwan (as part of a medley with *E Lili'u Ē*) from the recording KE'ALA'S MELE (Dancing Cat 38004) in a ***G6 Mauna Loa Tuning*** (D-G-D-E-G-D), sometimes called ***Maori Brown Eyes Tuning*** because the well-known piece, *Maori Brown Eyes*, is sometimes played in this tuning.

Sonny Chillingworth (under title *Kī Kaholu*) from the recording SONNY CHILLINGWORTH (Makaha Records 2014—out of print) in ***G Mauna Loa Tuning*** (D-G-D-D-G-D). ***Mauna Loa*** tunings have the characteristic of tuning the 1st & 2nd strings (the two thinnest) a fifth apart. This allows a player to play very sweet phrases in sixth intervals on the first two strings, rather than on the first and thicker third string (commonly used in ***Taro Patch***).

Gabby Pahinui from the recording PURE GABBY (Hula Records 567) in ***C Mauna Loa Tuning*** (C-G-E-G-A-E).

Gabby Pahinui from the recording THE HISTORY OF SLACK KEY GUITAR (Hana Ola Records 24000) in ***C Mauna Loa Tuning*** (C-G-E-G-A-E).

Sonny Chillingworth from an upcoming recording on Dancing Cat Records in ***G Mauna Loa Tuning*** (D-G-D-D-G-D).

A similar sounding song is Ray Kāne's *Wai'anae Slack Key Hula* from the recording PUNAHELE (Dancing Cat 38001) in ***Taro Patch.***

Lei 'Ohu

Gabby Pahinui from the recording GABBY ("The Brown Album," Panini Records 1002) in a ***C Wahine Tuning*** (C-G-E-G-B-E), tuned down to key of B and fingered in keys of E & C, which due to the tuning down a half step actually sound in the keys of E♭ and B. This tuning is often called ***Hi'ilawe*** or ***Gabby's Hi'ilawe Tuning*** (see notes to *Hi'ilawe*).

Cyril Pahinui from the recording 6 & 12 STRING SLACK KEY (Dancing Cat 38010) in ***C Major Tuning*** (C-G-E-G-C-E), tuned down to the key of A. This C major tuning is called ***Atta's C*** because it was recorded first and most prominently by the late great slack key guitarist Leland "Atta" Isaacs, Sr. (1929-1983) of the celebrated Isaacs family.

Led Ka'apana & Bob Brozman for an upcoming recording on Dancing Cat Records with both slack key and acoustic steel guitars in ***Taro Patch*** (D-G-D-G-B-D).

Maikaʻi Ka Makani O Kohala

Keola Beamer from the upcoming recording KOLONAHE (FROM THE GENTLE WIND) on Dancing Cat Records in the ***F Wahine Tuning*** (C-F-C-G-C-E).

Ozzie Kotani from the recording KANI KĪ HŌʻALU (Dancing Cat 38013) in ***Taro Patch***.

Paʻahana

Sonny Chillingworth (as part of a medley with *Moana Chimes*) from the recording ENDLESSLY (Dancing Cat 38027) in ***Taro Patch*** tuning (D-G-D-G-B-D).

Sonny Chillingworth (as part of a medley with *Moana Chimes*) from the recording WAIMEA COWBOY (Mahalo Records 4011) in ***Taro Patch***.

Sonny Chillingworth (as part of *Slack Key Medley*) from the recording HAWAIʻI ALOHA (Waikiki Records 107—compilation album with 2 tracks by Sonny Chillingworth) in ***Taro Patch.***

Led Ka'apana & Bob Brozman from the recording KĪKĀ KILA MEETS KĪ HŌʻALU (Dancing Cat 38031) with both slack key and acoustic steel guitars in ***Taro Patch.***

Dennis Kamakahi from upcoming recording on Dancing Cat Records in a ***C Mauna Loa Tuning*** (C-G-E-G-A-E).

Pu'u O Hulu

Keola Beamer (recorded under the title *Kaula 'Ili*) from the recording MAUNA KEA–WHITE MOUNTAIN JOURNAL (Dancing Cat 38011) in ***D Wahine Tuning*** (D-A-D-F♯-A-C♯, from lowest pitched string to highest).

Sonny Chillingworth (under the title *Kaula 'Ili*) from the recording SONNY SOLO (Dancing Cat 38005) in the G Major Tuning (D-G-D-G-B-D), often called ***Taro Patch*** tuning.

Kahumoku Bros. (Moses & George) (under the title *Kaula 'Ili*) from the recording SWEET AND SASSY–HAWAIIAN SLACK KEY STYLING, VOL. 1 (Kahumoku Brothers 1005—out of print) in ***Taro Patch***, tuned down to the key of F.

Moses Kahumoku (under the title *Kaula 'Ili*) from the recording HO'OKUPU "THE GIFT" (Dancing Cat 38023) in ***Taro Patch***, playing in keys of G & C.

Led Ka'apana from an upcoming recording on Dancing Cat Records in ***Modified C Wahine Tuning*** (C-G-D-G-B-D), often called ***Leonard's C*** because it is used very prominently by the great slack key guitarist Leonard Kwan.

Sase

Keola Beamer from the recording MAUNA KEA–WHITE MOUNTAIN JOURNAL (Dancing Cat 38011) in ***C Wahine Tuning*** (C-G-D-G-B-E), often called *Keola's C* because Keola Beamer is the one to have recorded most prominently in it.

Leonard Kwan from the recording THE OLD WAY (Tradewinds Records TS-1128) in ***Taro Patch***.

Sweet Leilehua

Atta Isaacs from the recordings ATTA ("The Orange Album," Tradewinds Records 1126—out of print) and (same version) TWO SLACK KEY GUITARS (Tradewinds Records 1124) in ***C Major Tuning*** (C-G-E-G-C-E).

Sonny Chillingworth from upcoming recording on Dancing Cat Records in ***Taro Patch***.

Ua Like Nō A Like

Led Ka'apana & Bob Brozman from the recording KĪKĀ KILA MEETS KĪ HŌ'ALU (Dancing Cat 38031) with Led playing slack key guitar in a ***C Wahine Tuning*** (C-G-D-G-B-D), and Bob playing acoustic steel guitar in G Major Tuning ***(Taro Patch)*** (D-G-D-G-B-D), playing in C.

'Ūlili Ē

Keola Beamer from the recording MAUNA KEA–WHITE MOUNTAIN JOURNAL (Dancing Cat 38011) in ***Modified C Wahine Tuning (Leonard's C)*** (C-G-D-G-B-D).

Dennis Kamakahi from the recording 'OHANA (Dancing Cat 38043) in ***C Mauna Loa Tuning*** (C-G-E-G-A-E), tuned down to B♭.

Wehiwehi 'Oe

George Kuo, from the recording HAWAIIAN TOUCH, (Dancing Cat 38026) with Barney Isaacs and George Kuo. George plays in ***Modified C Wahine*** (C-G-D-G-B-D, also called ***Leonard's C***); Barney plays acoustic steel in A minor 7th tuning (C-E-G-A-C-E).

Titles not listed either have not yet been released as recordings by slack key guitarists or are unavailable at this time.

Resources

Recordings

Due to renewed interest in *kī hō'alu* and Hawaiian music, it has become easier to find a good selection of recordings in almost every major Mainland city. Mail order sources include Harry's Music, 3457 Wai'alae Avenue, Honolulu, HI 96806, and the House of Music, 1415 Ala Moana Blvd. #1116, Honolulu, HI 96814. On the Internet, The Hawaiian Music Island (www.mele.com) is an excellent source of both recordings and books.

GABBY PAHINUI
Slack key's most famous and influential artist recorded a number of ground-breaking albums, both as a bandleader and as a member of The Sons of Hawai'i and the Maile Serenaders. All of his recordings are a delight. Some recommended examples:
Gabby Pahinui Hawaiian Band, Volumes 1 & 2 (Panini Records PS 1007 and PS 1008)
Pure Gabby (Hula Records CD HS 567)
Music of Old Hawai'i (Hula Records CDHS 506)
Hawai'i's favorite Slack Key and Steel Guitar Instrumentals, Volume 2 (Hula Records CDHS 531)

ATTA ISAACS
Two Slack Key Guitars—A Livin' on a Easy (w/ Gabby Pahinui) (Tradewinds Records TW 1124)

RAY KĀNE
Wa'ahila (Dancing Cat Records 38002)
Punahele (Dancing Cat Records 08022 38001)

SONNY CHILLINGWORTH
Waimea Cowboy (Mahalo Records MSC 4011)
Sonny Solo (Dancing Cat Records 08022 38005)

LEONARD KWAN
Ke'ala's Mele (Dancing Cat Records 08022 38004)
The following recordings are extremely hard to find, sometimes they show up in used record stores.
Slack Key (Tradewinds Records TS 103)
The Old Way (Tradewinds Records TS 1128)

LEDWARD KA'APANA
Waltz of the Wind (Dancing Cat Records 38016)
Led Live, Solo (Dancing Cat Records 08022 38008)
Also look for recordings as part of the groups HUI 'OHANA and I KONA.

KEOLA BEAMER
Kolonahe—From the Gentle Wind (Dancing Cat Records 8022-38047-2)
Mauna Kea—White Mountain Journal (Dancing Cat Records 08022 38006)
Moe'uhane Kīkā—Tales from the Dream Guitar (Dancing Cat Records 08022 38006)
Wooden Boat (Dancing Cat Records 08022 380024)

In addition, look for recordings by Ozzie Kotani, George Kuo, Cyril Pahinui, James "Bla" Pahinui, Moses Kahumoku and George Kahumoku, Jr., Sunday Mānoa, Peter Moon, Leabert Lindsey, John Keawe and many other fine Hawaiian musicians.

Instructional Videos

KEOLA BEAMER
The Art of Hawaiian Slack Key Guitar (Homespun Video, P.O. Box 694, Woodstock, N.Y. 12498. (1-800-TAPES) Also available from www.kbeamer.com.

RAY KĀNE
Slack Key Guitar (Kī Hō'alu) Instructional Video
The Slack Key Secrets of Ray Kāne
(available from www.kbeamer.com)

Books

OZZIE KOTANI
Guitar Playing Hawaiian Style, Kī Hō'alu, *Volume 1* (with cassette)
(Native Books, available from www.kbeamer.com)

HAL KINNAMAN
Teach Yourself Slack Key Guitar, with cassette
Early Slack Key Melodies, with cassette
(Slack Key Publications, PO Box 635, Kalāheo, KI 96741)

LEONARD KWAN
Slack Key Instruction Book
(Tradewinds Recording, available from Elderly Music, PO Box 14210, Lansing, MI 48901)

KEOLA BEAMER
Keola Beamer Teaches Hawaiian Slack Key Guitar (Homespun)
First Method for Hawaiian Slack Key Guitar (Beamer Hawaiiana, Inc.)
Hawaiian Slack Key Guitar (Oak Publications)
(Though both books are out of print, they occasionally turn up in used book stores.)

SAMUEL ELBERT AND NOELANI MAHOE
Nā Mele O Hawai'i Nei—101 Hawaiian Songs
University of Hawai'i Press
2840 Kolowalu St
Honolulu. HI 96822
This wonderful book contains the words to many of the songs you have studied. Highly recommended.

Guide to Pronouncing Hawaiian

The Hawaiians had no written alphabet until one was created by the missionaries slightly over 150 years ago. To someone unfamiliar with the language, the multiple vowels and long words may appear daunting at first. Just remember to pronounce every letter and to break up long words into smaller parts, and you'll do fine.

Most glossaries will tell you that there are twelve letters in the Hawaiian alphabet: the five vowels A, E, I, O and U; and seven consonants: H, K, L, M, N, P and W. This is OK as far as it goes, but the spoken language is considerably richer. Certain sounds were difficult for English speakers to shoehorn into the common alphabet; one confusing example is the letter W. Depending on where it falls in a word, and depending on where in the Islands the speaker lives, this letter may sound like a V, like a W, or like something in between.

The situation isn't confined to this single consonant, as a quick look at two early spellings of the name of the Islands will illustrate: *Havaiki* and *Owyhee.*

Vowels are pronounced similar to Spanish. The macron changes the vowel slightly, making it sound longer.

a as in *far*
ā as in *father*
e as in *bet*
ē like *ay* in *pay*
i, ī like *ee* in *see*
o ō as in *sole*
u, ū like *oo* in *moon*

The vowel pairs: ai, ae, ao, au, ei, eu, iu, and oi. Pronounce each letter individually, with a slight stress on the first. The second letter is pronounced softly. They differ from the English diphthong; so *Maika'i* is *ma-ee-KA-'ee*, not *MY-KY.*

The consonants are pronounced almost as they are in English, but generally softer.

W is a special case:
following ***i*** or ***e***, pronounce it as a soft ***v.***
as the initial letter, or following **a**; pronounce it as either a ***w*** or a soft ***v.***
following ***u*** and ***o***; usually pronounced as ***w***, but sometimes as a soft ***v.***

The ***'okina*** or ***'u'ina*** (') is another difficult sound for English speakers to grasp. This symbol represents a glottal stop, an abrupt cessation of breath similar to the sound between the words in the exclamation: Uh-oh! The *'u'ina* is a consonant, failure to pronounce it changes the meaning of the word, such as *pau* = finished, and *pa'u* = soot, smudge.

As a general rule, accent the next to the last syllable in short words. Break up longer words into pieces to help find the stress; so *Keolaokalani* becomes *Ke-ola-o-ka-lani.*

It's really not too difficult if you take it slow. Sort of like life, really.

Keola Beamer

"The Quintessential Master of the Slack Key Guitar Style"
—New York Times

Keola Beamer is a master of Hawaiian artistic expression. The fascinating history of his family can be traced back to the 15th century, to such distinguished *kūpuna* (ancestors) as Ahiakūmai Ki'eki'e, queen of the island of Hawai'i, one of the *kapu* (sacred) twins born of Kame'eiamoku, favored wife of Kamehameha Nui. In traditional Hawaiian society, *ali'i* (royalty) such as these recognized that sounded words possess *mana* (spiritual power). They encouraged musical expression as a way to preserve information and communicate with one another and the gods.

Throughout the generations, the Beamers have been involved in the performing arts. In the 20th century, they have produced a number of influential performers, composers and teachers. Keola's great grandmother, Helen Kapuailohia Desha Beamer (1882–1952), was one of Hawai'i's most prolific and accomplished composers. She was also a skilled dancer whose grace left a lasting imprint on the *hula* (Hawaiian dance). Her granddaughter, Winona (Nona) Kapuailohia Beamer, is Keola's mother. A noted chanter, composer, and singer, Nona is revered for her scholarship and accomplishments in the education of Native Hawaiian children.

Keolamaikalani Breckenridge Desha Beamer carries the legacy into the 21st century. "My family is serious about music," Keola says. "We came from a history of oral tradition in which music was a central component. Our genealogies, land boundaries, and navigational information were all in the chant form. We are now just beginning to realize the wealth of that knowledge and how so much of it has been lost. We are finally making some serious footholds in regaining some of these meanings and incorporating them in our own lives."

Keola has played guitar, piano, and *'ohe hano iho* (bamboo nose flute) since he was very young. He studied *hula* and sang in glee clubs while attending Kamehameha School for children of Hawaiian ancestry in Honolulu. Keola was an active teacher of *kī hō'alu* (slack key guitar) in the 1970's and compiled the first comprehensive teaching manual on the subject, ***Hawaiian Slack Key Guitar*** (Oak Publications, New York). His contributions to slack key during the 70's began to spark public interest in *kī hō'alu*, launching a statewide revival of the tradition. His teaching continues today with an instructional video, **The Art Of Hawaiian Slack Key Guitar** (Homespun Tapes, New York). Keola is especially noted for his ability to recontextualize ancient Hawaiian *mele* (songs) into contemporary settings, in which he has created a style uniquely his own.

Keola's recording history has been a series of ground-breaking releases, beginning in 1972 with the solo slack key album **Hawaiian Slack Key Guitar In The Real Old Style**. That LP that was the catalyst for the revival of *kī hō'alu*. His 1978 release, **Honolulu City Lights** was the largest selling recording in the history of Hawaiian music. In 1994, **Wooden Boat**, Keola's first release on the Dancing Cat label, became the first Hawaiian music LP ever to reach the top 15 on the Billboard World Music

Charts. His second release, **Moe'uhane Kīkā—Tales From The Dream Guitar** also reached the Top 15, as did his third release, **Mauna Kea—White Mountain Journal.**

Keola's live performance entitled **Mo'olelo—Tales From The Dream Guitar** embodies the magical "other worldliness" of this melodic language of dreams, his unique and polished style of musicianship skillfully accentuating the stories that his songs tell about the culture. **Mo'olelo—Tales From The Dream Guitar** is a three dimensional overture combining the elements of *Mele* (song), *Hula* (dance), and *Oli* (chant) with native instruments and Hawaiian folklore.

Mauna Kea—White Mountain Journal, is an instrumental diary of Keola's upbringing. He was raised by his Hawaiian family on the slopes of *Mauna Kea*, the White Mountain, by the quiet light of kerosene lamps and the distant sound of the *pueo* (Hawaiian owl). It is a warm recollection of experiences, life stories, and observations from this current of time.

Be sure to check out Keola's web page at http://www.kbeamer.com for more information such as tour dates, instruction, family folklore, and much more.

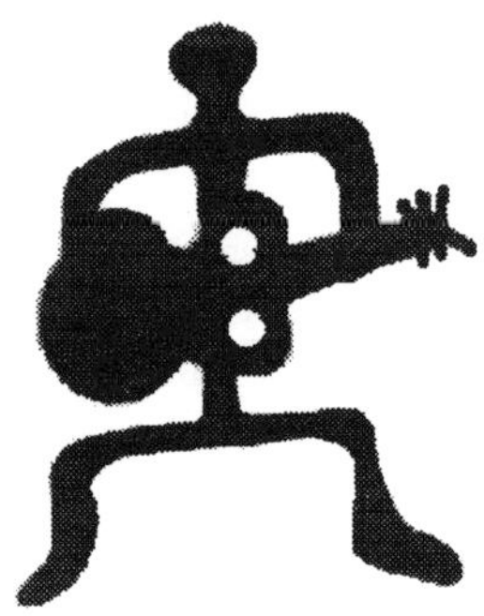

Keola Beamer

Selected Discography

Kolonahe—From the Gentle Wind
Dancing Cat Records (8022-38047-2)

Mauna Kea—White Mountain Journal
Dancing Cat Records (8022-38011-2)

Moe'uhane Kīkā—Tales From The Dream Guitar
Dancing Cat Records (08022-38006-2)

Wooden Boat
Dancing Cat Records (08022-38024-2)

Hawaiian Slack Key Guitar In The Real Old Style
Music of Polynesia (MOP 22000)

Sweet Maui Moon
Paradise Productions (SCD980)

(with other artists)

The Golden Lehua Tree—Stories and Music from the Heart of Hawai'i's Beamer Family
Narrated by Nona Beamer
Starscape Music (SM 96112)

On A Starry Night Selected Windham Hill Artists
Windham Hill Records (01934-11213-2)

Summer Solstice Keola Beamer & George Winston with Selected Windham Hill Artists
Windham Hill Records (01934-11239-2)

A Winter's Solstice V Keola Beamer & George Winston with Selected Windham Hill Artists
Windham Hill Records (1934-11174-2)

Kī Hō'alu Christmas Selected Dancing Cat Artists
Dancing Cat Records (08022-38006-2)

Hawaiian Slack Key Guitar Masters Selected Dancing Cat Artists
Dancing Cat Records (08022-38032-2)

KEOLA AND KAPONO BEAMER

Honolulu City Lights
Paradise Productions (SLP808)

Tahiti Holiday
Paradise Productions (SLP991)

"Big Wednesday" Soundtrack
From the Motion Picture ***Big Wednesday***
Copyright 1978 Warner Bros. Studios, several pieces of music on the soundtrack, including the movie's theme song

Keola and Kapono Beamer
Tantalus Records (TR2453)

This Is Our Island Home—We Are Her Sons
Music of Polynesia (MOP 22300)

Mark Nelson

Multi-instrumentalist Mark Nelson has carved a unique niche for himself as an entertainer, musician and educator. His deep love and understanding of traditional music led him to the mastery of several different musical idioms, ranging from old time western music to Celtic to R & B. In a career that began well before he was able to drive, he has performed everywhere from street corners to hay barns to festivals to the concert stage in the US, Europe and Canada. He once worked as a banjo playing gorilla in Dublin, but that's a different story.

Mark's mastery of the Appalachian dulcimer won him a first place in the National Dulcimer Championships in 1979. He has appeared at such prestigious venues as "A Prairie Home Companion", the Letterkenny, Ireland International Folk Festival, and the halftime show for the Skagway, Alaska Girls Junior Varsity Basketball Team. Though his parents tell him he played *'ukulele* as a child, he doesn't remember.

Mark lives in Southern Oregon's Applegate Valley with his wife Annie and various four-footed friends, where he divides his time between studio work, writing, and watching the trees grow. He may be reached in care of Acme Arts, P.O. Box 967, Jacksonville, OR 97530.

Selected Discography

Autumn
Wizmak Productions (W579-33CD)

The Faery Hills
Wizmak Productions (W579-34CD)

Southern Light
Flying Fish Records (FF70405)

After the Morning
Kicking Mule Records (KM 241)

The Rights of Man
Kicking Mule Records (KM 218)

Books

You Can Teach Yourself to Make Homemade Musical Instruments Mel Bay Publications
The Complete Collection of Celtic Music for Appalachian Dulcimer Mel Bay Publications
Scottish Airs and Ballads for Dulcimer Mel Bay Publications

Recording Credits

Keola Beamer—HAWAIIAN SLACK KEY GUITAR

Akāka Falls, Aunty Alice Nāmakelua Slack Key, Tiare Tahiti, Kī Hō'alu Mischief, 'Ūlili Ē, Hi'ilawe, Kāhuli Aku

Mark Nelson—HAWAIIAN SLACK KEY GUITAR

Akāka Falls, Aunty Alice Nāmakelua Slack Key, Tiare Tahiti, Kī Hō'alu Mischief, Ahi Wela. 'Alekoki/Hula O Makee, Sase/Hilo March, Matt's Bounce, Wehiwehi 'Oe, Sweet Leilehua, Isalei, Ua Like Nō A Like, Ka Makani 'Olu'olu, Kī Hō'alu

Slippers the cat—inappropriate playfulness and cable mischief
stupid mynah birds—scolding, scolding, leaking into audio tracks

Recorded at
BUMBYE STUDIOS
Unda da Mango Tree,
three houses past da park,
Lahaina, Maui, Hawai'i.
Engineer—**Beatrice Laulauna'ole**
and
ACME ARTS RECORDING
Applegate Valley, Oregon
Engineer—**Buzz Faders**

Keola Beamer appears on this recording courtesy of **Dancing Cat Records**.

Keola makes music on beautiful double-holed koa guitars, hand-crafted by **Steve Grimes of Grimes Guitars P.O. Box 537, Kula, HI 96790. (808) 878 2076www.maui.net/~grimer**

Keola uses **John Pearse Strings** exclusively. **1-800-235-3302 www.jpstrings.com**

For more information on the music of **Keola Beamer**, slack key instruction, video clips, and much more, surf to his web page at **http://www.kbeamer.com**

Publishing Information

Photo–Annie Dempsey

Keola Beamer and Mark Nelson
Lahaina, Maui 1998